Leadership Strategies:
Achieving Personal and Professional Success

Ronald Menaker, EdD, FACMPE

Medical Group Management Association

Library of Congress Cataloging-in-Publication Data
Menaker, Ronald.
  Leadership strategies : achieving personal and professional success / Ronald Menaker, EdD, FACMPE, MBA, CPA.
     pages cm
  Includes bibliographical references and index.
  ISBN 978-1-56829-433-9
  1. Medicine--Practice--Management. 2. Group medical practice--Management. 3. Leadership. I. Title.
  R728.M476 2013
  610.68--dc23
                              2013030952

Item #8707
ISBN: 978-1-56829-433-9

Printed in the United States of America
10 9 8 7 6 5 4 3 2 1

Dedication

During the passages and transitions of my leadership journey, I have been fortunate to have been inspired by both an individual *and* an organization that have had a profound impact on my leadership development. They helped me learn that by helping others, my life is more meaningful. My dreams are becoming real as a result. Therefore, this book is dedicated, with sincere appreciation, to both Frederick (Fritz) Wenzel and the Mayo Clinic.

Frederick (Fritz) Wenzel

Fritz entered my life in the spring of 1985. Since then, I have learned from his leadership mastery as a scientist, manager, leader, teacher, advisor, consultant, writer, editor, presenter, mentor, philanthropist, volunteer, and friend. I am very fortunate to have him as a guide.

The Mayo Clinic

William J. Mayo, one of the founders of the Mayo Clinic (Rochester, Minn.), believed that there was a "spirit of the Clinic." The primary value of "the needs of the patient come first" and the mission, "to inspire hope and contribute to health and well-being by providing the best care to every patient through integrated clinical practice, education and research," provide the foundation for Mayo Clinic leaders. The values of respect, compassion, integrity, healing, teamwork, excellence, innovation, and stewardship are expressed continuously with inspiration by the physician, scientist, and allied health team.

Contents

Preface

After completing graduate school and starting a career, it was very apparent that my formal schooling provided a firm foundation to begin employment, but there was a need to develop my skills in self-management, including stress management and building relationships with others. To improve these abilities, I started to journalize my thoughts, inspirations, and frustrations. I carried a journal so I could capture important reflections and leadership concepts at the moment they occurred. Entries involved observations, stressors, concerns, successes, and failures. Journalizing provided an immediate opportunity to capture the thought, emotion, or inspiration.

Writing these entries was cathartic. As a manager, I am often confronted with high-conflict and/or high-risk situations. I was frequently tempted to act defensively or negatively, but I also knew that the release of negative emotion often causes damage. The journal allowed release of emotion in a positive and private way.

Sample Journal Entry

September 23: The importance of relationships and values was clearly proven with the events of September 11. President Bush had one set of initiatives before the disaster. Following 9/11, he had different issues that redefined his priorities but that still required strong relationships to accomplish the job.

The journal also became a tool of lifelong learning. It helped me capture moments of creativity and inspiration so I could use them as intellectual capital to enrich my organization. I also recorded reflections that occurred during times of disappointment, rejection, or depression. A friend once told me that good judgment comes from experience, and experience sometimes stems from bad judgment. If I could capture the wisdom gained from bad judgment, it would help me rise to the next level of leadership.

As I gained experience, my focus and journal entries shifted from growing and self-learning to developing relationships and leading others. Over time, I extended the learning to achieve organizational excellence. While the early years were relatively stress free, the responsibilities of marriage, children, and home ownership combined with more stress and responsibilities at work prompted the realization of finding a healthy balance of work and life. As my responsibilities shifted, I felt a continuous need to maintain the leadership journal.

One of the questions I have asked throughout my journey is: Who are the leaders in the enterprise and why are they the leaders? In my definition, leaders are not just the individuals in positions of leadership. Rather, they are the "go to" individuals who can be counted on, who are approachable, and who have developed and used their leadership strategies effectively. I recorded my insights and inspirations from observing these leaders.

The concept of this book on leadership was first formulated in the fall of 1976 after 120 journal entries had been posted. At that time, I believed there might be a benefit to sharing these thoughts with others. During the next 37 years, I recorded more than 2,200 entries on a variety of topics. The journal entries were inspired by three sources: my own experiences, readings from various literature, and teaching others. My experiences provided a foundation for learning and identifying strategies. Additional ideas came from reading several hundred books, whether they were academically inclined or from practitioners in the field. The third source of ideas came from teaching accounting, organization development, and leadership strategies in three master of business administration (MBA) programs.

During the process of reviewing the journal entries for this book, I realized they were written as strategies in a logical sequence from which I developed an integrated leadership model. The model presents the four aspects in a leader's career:

1. Leading Self through Learning;

2. Leading Others by Developing Relationships;

3. Leading Organizations by Achieving Excellence; and

4. Achieving a Healthy Work–Life Integration and Synergy.

Under each aspect and organized by topic in the model that follows are the strategies and inspirations that have helped me succeed in my career and life. Leading self utilizes learning and reflection as a foundation. It includes strategies to address anger, frustration, and anxiety and discusses the importance of reflection, humility, optimism, patience, resilience, and confidence. Leading others has professionalism as a base and utilizes listening and presence in order to work through the inherent conflict found when working with others. Strategies helpful for relationship building include conflict management, valuing diversity and inclusiveness, being assertive, and maintaining a perspective.

Integrated Leadership Model

©2013 Ronald Menaker

Leading self and others serve as the foundation to what we as leaders are expected to do: achieve organizational excellence for long-term success. Strategies or reflections address the power of having vision, setting priorities and reducing noise, utilizing organizational skills, taking initiative, solving problems, and managing change. Achieving results, including being persistent and accountable, is the concluding orientation for attaining excellence.

Personal sustainability is not possible without a vital fourth area: work–life integration and synergy. The pressures of self and relationship management as well as a career can easily cause damage to oneself, creating imbalances that result in poor health, either emotional, physical, or both. Accordingly, the fourth chapter addresses strategies, including relaxation and accepting reality, to achieve personal health and wealth in the leadership journey. In this case, wealth is a "psychic" wealth of leading a meaningful life of contribution that is consistent with personal values.

The unprecedented rate of change in the healthcare industry (and other industries) has resulted in enormous leadership challenges to improve the effectiveness and efficiency of organizations and their success at implementing changes. The industry needs leaders with the skills and strategies to successfully carry organizations through these challenging times. At the same time, leaders need to manage themselves as they manage their organizations to sustain a high level of effectiveness.

The approach to achieving success is to manage and lead self, others, and organizations while maintaining work–life integration and synergy. This book supports this integrated model of leadership with insights and strategies in all four aspects. It is intended for frequent use with each chapter divided into topics that can be referenced time and time again when leaders are faced with these pressing challenges. Questions for reflection at the end of each chapter provide an opportunity for readers to consider their own strategies for managing each topic area. Leaders should see organizational, professional, and personal benefits from reading and deploying the insights and strategies journalized during 37 years of leading others and 20 years of teaching graduate students.

The reader may already know and practice some of the insights, but there will be many strategies that leaders need to be reminded of to put into practice. Additional insights will be new and will complement the reader's experiences and knowledge to enhance their leadership capability. This book is intended as a practical approach to sustainable personal and professional leadership with specific behavioral strategies.

The books listed in the bibliography provided many of my inspirations and insights. I hope they will also be helpful to you in developing your leadership capabilities.

Acknowledgments

Writing this book and pursuing a career in leadership development is a result of the tremendous support from my family and colleagues. I deeply appreciate the encouragement from the following groups and individuals while writing this manuscript:

- The Medical Group Management Association–American College of Medical Practice Executives (MGMA-ACMPE), who shared my enthusiasm for writing a book that would be a guide to anyone seeking to improve their leadership capabilities;

- Dr. Joseph Murphy, who provided the spark to start writing a leadership book;

- Mary Mourar, who partnered with me in crafting the wording that would be meaningful and helpful to readers. Mary, you helped turn my journal into a guide for others: thank you;

- Nicole Engler, who read chapters as they were being formulated and provided objective feedback;

- Karen Benassi, who maintained an order for the suggested readings and references;

- The MBA students over the past 20 years and the leadership at the University of St. Thomas Opus College of Business in Minnesota who provided inspiration that this book would be beneficial to leaders in healthcare and other industries;

- My colleagues at the Mayo Clinic, who provided administrative guidance initiating the process in the writing of the book and the modeling of inspirational leadership practices;

- My colleagues from MGMA-ACMPE, who reviewed and provided feedback on the book prior to publication, so that the finished product could be optimally helpful:
  - Alan J. Beason, MS, FACMPE, CEO/administrator, Cardiovascular Consultants, LLP, Shreveport, La.
  - Frederick J. Wenzel, FACMPE, Monona, Wis.
  - Tom Ludwig, RN, FACMPE, president and CEO, Forward Healthcare Solutions, LLC, McFarland, Wis.
  - William Henderson, FACMPE, administrator, The Neurology Group LLP, Albany, N.Y.
  - Warren C. White Jr., FACMPE, VP physician practices, Lakeland Healthcare, Saint Joseph, Mich.

A book can only be written with the support of family, my primary value. I acknowledge the love and support from:

- My wife, Linda Mansfield, the love of my life (LOML), who has lived my leadership journey with me: guiding me, providing honest feedback, teaching me those leadership lessons that can only come from a spouse;
- My children (Gregg, Nicole, Jess, and Ben) and their spouses, who have provided loving support, either directly in the preparation of the book or indirectly as the best children that a father could ask for;
- My brothers and sisters, who provide the love of an extended family; and
- Mike Menaker, my older brother, who guided me through adolescence and directed my education after our parents died at a premature age, a time when I could have taken the wrong road but was fortunate to find the right pathway. Mike, this book and my leadership journey has been accomplished on the foundation you provided.

With sincere appreciation,

Ronald Menaker

CHAPTER ONE

Leading Self through Learning

Integrated Leadership Model

**Leading Others:
Developing Relationships**

- Professionalism
- Listening
- Conflict
- Assertiveness
- Diversity and Inclusiveness
- Perspective

**Leading Self:
Through Learning**

- Reflection
- Humility
- Frustration, Anger, Anxiety
- Optimism and Patience
- Resilience and Confidence

**Work-Life
Integration
and
Synergy**

**Leading Organizations:
Achieving Excellence**

- Vision
- Priorities and Being Organized
- Initiative
- Problem Solving
- Change Management
- Achieving Results

©2013 Ronald Menaker

Learning

Leading self is the starting point for becoming an effective leader. Without the relevant knowledge, personal control, and confidence, an individual will not be effective in leading others or organizations. Knowledge and leadership competencies are developed through a lifetime of learning about the industry and about oneself. Essentially, leaders lead themselves by learning through experiences, reading from various sources, and engagement with others. The key is to learn from each opportunity.

Why Learning Is Important

Peter Vaill, one of the world's leading organizational development specialists, spoke of "a world of permanent whitewater," referencing the constant rapid change around us (Center for Creative Leadership 2003). He described the business environment characterized by chaos, ambiguity, uncertainty, competition, limited resources, and rapid technological changes. As a result, leaders need resilience and adaptability to understand and thrive in this environment. The stress of environmental change can have a positive or negative effect, depending on the choice of the leader.

Vaill knew learning can be a powerful strategy to address the constant change. One of his solutions for handling the permanent whitewater is for people to become "extremely effective learners" and "to approach learning as a way of being – not a separate activity or a task for becoming a leader" (Center for Creative Leadership 2003). Learning is especially important for someone beginning a career but has become a necessary leadership strategy throughout one's career.

Too often, people do not think about learning after they leave the education system, but learning is an ongoing effort, whether it occurs on the job, from peers or others around you, or through one's experiences. Think of continuous learning as a chance for *individual* improvement the way continuous quality improvement has become a strategy for *organizational* improvement. You should be constantly assessing whether you are learning, either from an experience, a peer or mentor, or from reading. The advantages and outcomes of lifelong learning are many and include:

- Establishing a foundation for future learning;
- Developing critical thinking skills;
- Learning a body of knowledge relevant to your career and future;
- Gaining leadership skills and competencies; and

- Adding to the industry's body of knowledge through scholarship.

Learning is not about having the answers; it is about having strategies to know when and how to obtain and apply new knowledge. Strategic thinking is important to identify strategies to achieve organizational goals. Strategic learning supports strategic thinking by identifying what needs to be learned. It is about asking the right questions: What is causing something to happen? What do I need to know to help me address this situation? Where do I go to obtain that knowledge? Am I making an assumption or developing an opinion? Do I need additional information or another opinion to confirm the assumption or opinion? How do I prepare for the future?

Learning is not about just facts and figures, it is also the knowledge or experience on how to address stressors, cope with frustration, overcome challenges, and listen to others. This type of learning requires personal reflection, managing negative emotions, and optimizing positive emotions. Learning from life's lessons will provide a resilience to address the challenges of life and the "whitewater environment." Learning can provide the power to succeed when life can take a turn for the worse.

Learning can also be thought of as a "conditioning" process. As athletes constantly work to maintain their physical and mental processes to win in competition, individuals can also condition themselves with lifelong learning to strive for excellence in the world of organizations. Lifelong learning might best be compared with training for and running marathons. There are many similarities:

- Training and running with others through teamwork provides the shared knowledge and mutual encouragement to persist toward a goal;
- Pacing helps maintain a resilience for continued learning and personal growth;
- Persistence builds strength and commitment to achieve the goal;
- Patience is knowing that desired results will come, gradually;

- Overcoming or pushing through obstacles, like the "runner's wall," that emerge from time to time is required to achieve success; and

- Enjoying the run and the journey is possible with appropriate training and having the right team for inspiration.

Strategies for Successful Learning

Learning comes from a variety of sources: books, mentors and peers, and oneself from accepting new challenges and reflecting on actions and decisions. Learning can also be inhibited by a variety of factors, such as previous experiences, habits, biases, prejudices, confrontations, stressors, and so forth.

Learning by Reading

Find the time to learn about leadership, your career field, and the latest news in business by reading and listening to experts in the field. Otherwise, you risk no longer having the competencies to succeed in the current environment and you may limit your sources of potential knowledge. Professional journals, books, conferences, and social media can all be utilized to learn from experts.

Reading leadership books and articles are outstanding strategies for development. Effectively, you are spending a few hours to incorporate an expert's years of learning into your leadership capability. Setting aside time to read can have a very high return on investment, as you are capitalizing on the experiences of others and considering how you can improve your effectiveness. You may take away only one or two ideas; however, they can become the difference between achieving the ordinary or the "extra" ordinary. Many of the ideas in the literature are just slight modifications, adaptations, or perspectives from the existing approach but can still make a large impact on you and your job. Also, the leadership books may be helpful for your personal as well as your professional life.

So, when you get frustrated, angry, bored, or stuck in a rut, read a book. A book can provide you with more tools for dealing with the negatives and stressors in life. It may inspire you to develop, learn, or relearn strategies that will move you to your vision.

Over time, the collective knowledge you gain will provide a leadership differential and advantage over others that choose to react in a less positive manner. Some of my favorite leadership books are listed in the bibliography at the end of this book.

Learning from Others

When evaluating learning opportunities, consider the personal and professional relationships that you have established over the years. Each individual has the potential of being an extended team member on your leadership journey. Many individuals in your life offer something to help you learn: older relatives who have had a lifetime of learning, as well as supervisors, colleagues, and mentors.

Seek their advice, listen to their opinions, and try to understand their viewpoints. Be ready to learn from their experiences.

Mentorship doesn't necessarily require an intensive one-on-one relationship. It can involve having a list of contacts for asking specific types of questions or for evaluating career opportunities. Mentors can be someone in the same field, but individuals in other fields can offer different yet pertinent insights.

The most significant mentor in my career was Frederick "Fritz" Wenzel, an experienced healthcare administrator and educator. I recall being interviewed by Fritz in 1985 when he was the executive director of Marshfield Clinic in Wisconsin. Over the next several decades, he introduced me to new opportunities to learn about medical group practice and teaching. For example, I was encouraged to give presentations at conferences, teach in graduate degree programs, and participate in professional association activities. These were usually experiences that would stretch my knowledge and challenge me, yet they provided the foundations for my enhanced learning and success. The leadership strategies I learned from Fritz were crucial for my development.

Colleagues are also critical as teachers and mentors, particularly when you are involved in new areas of discovery. Colleagues have different experiences, knowledge, and skills to contribute to projects and to share with you. The value of shared learning and hearing ideas from others is recognized in the use of project teams.

Teams can be a learning accelerator. Colleagues in high-performing teams are able to share their knowledge with you because each individual brings a unique set of experiences that can be shared with others. Collectively, the team can have much more competence and a shared learning experience if it achieves the "synergy" effect with the complement of experiences, skills, and personalities.

Learning from others will be enhanced if you have a lower affect or level of aggressiveness, as it will encourage more individuals to want to help you. High-affect personalities may intimidate others, make one less approachable, and discourage others from helping. Be aware of your personality and how you may appear to others to encourage interaction and shared learning.

Learning from Experiences

As you move through your career, be open to opportunities to gain new skills or competencies. There are hundreds of leadership skills, competencies, values, and virtues that need to be learned or acquired. One valuable step for accomplishing this is to accept new responsibilities or tasks. Each new project, task, or assignment provides an opportunity to learn new skills and the knowledge to become more proficient, both in your job and as a leader.

Accept new assignments to learn a new facet of the organization and industry. Most industries are complex with lots of interconnected parts. Gaining a broad system-level perspective will be helpful to develop a deeper understanding of the field and to anticipate emerging needs and trends. Learn what is going on with all stakeholders who interact with the industry.

For example, I participated in leadership development programs at both Marshfield Clinic and Mayo Clinic. Every few years, administrators like myself are asked to take on a new specialty or other new administrative assignment. These rotations provided an opportunity to work with new teams with different strengths, weaknesses, and opportunities. I experienced different subcultures along with new challenges previously unknown to me. As a result, I needed to learn new strategies to place in my leadership "toolbox." Collectively over many years, these "tools" have been helpful in choosing optimal strategies for different situations.

Taking on new challenges can push you beyond your current knowledge and, perhaps, skill level. The anxiety and stress that might be created should be channeled into learning what is needed to accomplish the new challenges and goals. Overcoming the challenge and stress of new assignments includes the following strategies:

- Ask for help; your network of colleagues, supervisors, and mentors are there to support you.
- Have confidence that you will find the resources to help you.
- Recognize that everything is a team effort.
- Remain calm.
- Know that this is a learning moment or opportunity, not a judgment call on your competence.
- Don't be concerned with some fear or anxiety; this can be motivating.
- Accept the learning curve that will enable you to get better, continuously.
- Don't bluff; know when you are out of your league.

An effective strategy is to break down the new assignment or challenge into manageable "chunks" with a visible goal. Address each piece in an appropriate priority, one at a time, even if they are coming at you in multiples. No surgeon would try too many organ transplants at the same time. Work through the process piece by piece, and celebrate the accomplishment of each step until the complete task or goal is completed.

Accepting a new position will be a greater challenge to overcome. Recognize that it takes time to learn what you did not know previously, to adjust to a new setting, and to meet new individuals. You may have to learn a new vocabulary or adapt to a new culture. It can even be similar to taking a new job in a foreign country; it takes time to learn the language and adapt to the nuances of a new culture. Over time, the stress of the new position will lessen as the amount of knowledge gained overcomes the amount of knowledge needed.

With more experience, after completing a few new tasks and assignments, you'll be able to use what you learned on new projects. Consider the previous projects, your accomplishments and failures. What worked and why? What did not work and why not? All experiences, both good and bad, provide valuable information that can be helpful in current and future situations.

Learning from Self

In addition to formal (degree) programs to further your education, there are several informal approaches and strategies to learning: journalizing to reflect on life experiences, teaching at universities/colleges, participating in leadership roles in professional associations, and so forth. All offer opportunities to gain new skills and competencies. Becoming involved in community and charitable organizations can offer learning opportunities and broaden your personal network. Keep an open mind on prospects new to your radar screen that will support continuous learning.

As mentioned previously, each new assignment or position offers new learning opportunities. The learning will be enhanced if you take the time to reflect on lessons after you've completed the assignment or task. Exhibit 1.1 offers advice for learning and opportunities for change.

As we will explore in the rest of this chapter, there is a cycle of learning, growth, maturity, and wisdom that will be at play as you move through your career. Several qualities facilitate this cycle: reflection, humility, optimism, patience, resilience, and confidence. Certain emotions can also hinder the cycle: frustration, anger, and anxiety. Be mindful of the importance of learning to gain this wisdom, to continue doing what is important, to stop doing what is no longer helpful or is damaging, and to identify those behaviors/experiences you should be initiating.

Reflection

Reflection is an important learning strategy. It involves taking the time to think, remember, or analyze. Reflection time is not idle time but rather it is learning time. It is an alternative to meditation, which is intended to quiet the mind, and is a time to direct your thoughts toward a purpose. Many leadership books reinforce the importance of reflection to stay in focus.

EXHIBIT 1.1 ■ Advice for Learning

Advice	Opportunity for Change
Don't be afraid of new ideas or challenges. Don't stick with old ideas out of fear that new ideas won't be as good or won't work.	Learn to be comfortable with change. Know that you will be shaking up the old and dealing with an unsettled period, but you'll become more comfortable over time. Recognize the opportunity to learn and the benefits of change.
Don't let established habits and responses lock your behavior. Habits have developed systems to support these habits. Comfortableness has been established, especially after a period of successes, and it may block the realization of the need to change.	Know when the previous learning is no longer helpful, that what you used to do is now causing damage. You should constantly assess whether a previous technique is working or if a new strategy and learning are required. An interesting metaphor of change is to view the need for "repotting." If you don't periodically repot a plant, it will struggle to grow. It is sometimes difficult to deliberately break the old pot in order to accomplish this transformation, but it may be required to achieve the ultimate results.
Don't be afraid of the unknown.	Become comfortable with the process of accepting the unknown and using learning to make it a known method. While it is natural to be uncomfortable with the ambiguity of not knowing an answer, the process of learning will provide greater clarity and opportunity for success.
Don't let unplanned speed bumps derail you. Don't let frustration, anger, disappointment, and other negative emotions overtake you at these times.	Rise to the challenge and develop a strategy, including learning, that will enable you to deal with the issues/challenges in a positive manner.
Don't let the "permanent whitewater" of a rapidly changing environment overwhelm you or leave you behind.	Much like your car needs occasional realignments, you will need to realign your thinking and strategies to accept and adapt to the changing environment.

Many purposes for reflection include:

- Reevaluating past actions;

- Evaluating the current situation;

- Considering new ideas, solutions, and actions, including their potential outcomes and consequences;

- Reviewing how resources are being used and whether a more effective use is possible;

- Evaluating interactions and relationships;

- Reconsidering the relevance of the current mission, vision, and strategies;

- Considering details that may be missed; and

- Appreciating those individuals who have helped you along the way.

The first step in reflection is simply "slowing down." You have to be going slow enough in order to reflect. You should quiet your mind and start to reflect. While the initial thoughts may appear random and/or superficial, this is what is on your mind. Direct your reflections to meaningful aspects of life, potential options, and different paths, or evaluate poor decisions.

The demands of the changing environment and fast pace of life can work against you in finding the time to reflect. But there will be times at work where there is a bit of a lull, including time between projects, when individuals are out on vacation, or late on Friday afternoons when many people have already gone home. Personal time, including at a coffee house or during a walk, can provide the opportunity for creating and contemplating new ideas. Utilize these times to reflect. Organizations can create time for group reflection during planned retreats.

No matter which time you choose, realize that it takes discipline to set aside time to reflect, and then use the time appropriately. This is not the time to get caught up in details or side-tracked but to focus on the purpose of the reflection time. It may be easier to continue working or keep the mind occupied on current tasks, but allowing time for reflection is vital to create a desirable future.

Values

Reflection time is an opportunity to pause and consider whether you are living your value system. Stating that something is part of your value system and living it are completely different. Living your values does not automatically happen, especially when you are being bombarded by the desires of others in an unfriendly environment of chaos, competition, and uncertainty. Living a values-based life will more likely occur when you take time to slow down, reflect, and assess what is going on.

Values are crucial life factors, as they are the foundation for our behavior, our ethical fabric, and our vision and goals. Values are the guides to how priorities are established and what importance is given to each. Writing them down will serve you well so that momentary seducers of your attention are mindfully considered. Sharing values with others is helpful so that they can understand what is providing the motivation for your actions. You can then inquire about their values so that you can demonstrate leadership by helping others on their journey.

Strategies for Reflection

Journalizing

Keeping a leadership journal is an effective strategy for reflecting and self-improvement. It is easy to do with limited resources or time, and can be done anytime with a variety of devices ranging from pen and paper to an iPad or laptop. Ideas, thoughts, and inspirations can be captured at the moment they come to you or later, after consideration. Captured thoughts can be for immediate use or over time as other situations arise. You can review the journal entries periodically to reflect on past thoughts and actions, and to determine if leadership and management competencies are being developed.

Journalizing can provide a cathartic relief to manage negative emotions by allowing you to express frustration, anger, anxiety, and so forth in a manner that is not displayed to others. Writing about the emotions and the reasons behind them can help in identifying solutions to handle the negative emotions and deal with the situation in a more positive manner.

Reflecting on the Past

While reflecting, think about what happened in a past circumstance and ask how the situation developed. Organize the sequence of phenomena that occurred; identify the cause and effect. Reevaluate past actions to assess whether they added value to accomplish the desired goals. Consider alternative responses that could have been employed and what might have brought about the desired results. Keep an open mind to think beyond the past action and the confines of known habits.

Use a reflective "after action review" to learn something new or different, especially after completing new tasks or assignments. Think through each situation to identify what can be learned from it and what might have been done differently. While successes are easier to react to and reflect on, it likely will be the disappointments or failures that provide better lessons. Always identify a positive that can be gained from the negative situation.

"Things happen for a reason" is a phrase you may have heard many times. The leadership challenge is to find out why – by asking questions, engaging in dialogue, and framing conversations to build relationships. Use reflection to consider each problem, challenge, or goal as a puzzle. Build the foundation of understanding by using good construction principles, and let the cement cure before trying to build on the foundation.

A meaningful example of using reflection as a strategy occurred for me when I was suddenly "in transition" between jobs. This led to several months of emotional soul searching while in outplacement. I used this opportunity to think deeply about my values and how I wanted to spend the rest of my career. The end result was accepting a position that was much more aligned with my interests, talents, and passion.

During reflection of past actions, it may help to imagine you've taken a seat in the "balcony" and are watching a play of the past, evaluating the action as it unfolds. Why were those decisions made? What was the response? How are you and the other players interacting? What if the lines were changed? How could it be rewritten for future performances?

Most religions have a time for reflection, often as the new year begins. This provides a regular opportunity to reflect on what may have gone well or poorly and to forgive others or yourself. The new year is a renewal that all individuals need in the cycle of life, with its ups and downs. Life is challenging, yet there are benefits to using these opportunities to take a new turn to create the future.

Reflecting on the Current

Reflecting on current issues and decisions enables you to consider the actions you are about to take and their consequences. This is when you can mindfully consider changes that otherwise may have been missed. Too often we're locked into automation and taking actions or making decisions through habit and inertia. Use reflection to consider if you're acting out of habit. Is this the right action for this situation or has the environment changed and a different tactic is needed?

Reflecting on the current situation enables you to evaluate and determine if results are being achieved as planned and desired. Review current actions in terms of their faithfulness to the organization's mission, vision, and values. Assess the strategies to consider adjustments or new ideas that could improve the results. Reflection can also provide an opportunity to identify how resources are being deployed and relationships are being developed and if they can be enhanced.

Being reflective will provide an opportunity to think at a higher level, to evaluate what the various forces are that are influencing results. Use the opportunity to look at the deep system issues, to look for the root causes through the symptoms, to ask "why" several times. These strategies will reduce the likelihood of taking actions that only temporarily resolve the problems.

Taking time for reflection can be particularly helpful when facing recurring problems or disappointments. It may be that you are using the wrong approach or strategy; don't have the necessary processes or resources; have an inadequate team; or don't have the necessary skills, desires, or interest. Take the time to evaluate what is going on, with a mindfulness that you may need to change something.

EXHIBIT 1.2 ■ Advice for Reflection

Advice	Opportunity for Change
Don't get caught up in the need for rapid response.	Speed is important, but so is direction. To go very fast in the wrong direction is not productive. Reflection involves slowing down to evaluate and confirm that you're heading in the right direction.
Don't wait for project end or year-end evaluations to reflect on actions and decisions. You'll only catch errors after they've happened.	Use reflection as part of a constant recalibration process as events occur to stop errors before they happen.
Don't let yourself become overly frustrated with a particular issue. By focusing on your frustration and the negative, you may be losing perspective on what is going well.	Use reflection for an objective assessment of what is going right in evaluating the frustrating challenges and stressors that are occupying your mind.
Don't dwell on small, lower-priority issues. There is merit to "Don't sweat the small stuff," as described in *Don't Sweat the Small Stuff at Work* by Richard Carlson (1998).	Reflection provides a vehicle to stay focused and to redirect the mind away from less important issues. Reflection time is an opportunity to remember important issues that may have been dislodged from work plans.
Don't let reflections become overly negative or reinforce a poor self-image. There is no benefit in beating yourself up by dwelling on the negative.	Take responsibility for your decisions, learn from them, even from the colossal mistakes, and then move on. Seek affirmations about what you are doing and how you will learn from the past.
Don't let reflection time serve as whining sessions or let yourself take the role of victim.	These thoughts will trap you into the negative instead of looking for alternatives. Direct your mind to look for the positive or identify how behavior can be changed for the better. Use the time to learn, improve, refocus, and push forward toward goals.

Reflecting can also play a role in avoiding burnout. Just like carpal tunnel syndrome and other injuries that are the result of constantly using the same muscles the same way, we can also burn out if we do the same thing the same way. Consider finding new ways of doing things and new approaches in order to avoid the wear and tear on the mind and maintain a high level of performance.

Reflecting will bring up ideas that are a great first step. Ideas then need to be acted on. This requires assertiveness, courage, and commitment. *Someday* is not a day of the week. Develop a plan, write it down, commit to taking actions frequently, hold yourself accountable, monitor for success, and adapt the plan if necessary. Exhibit 1.2 offers more ideas for reflection.

Humility

Humility is a desirable attribute to develop. Early in a career, this can be difficult as you are seeking promotions and trying to establish a "name" for yourself. The desire to be noticed and to get "credit" for your accomplishments is understandable. However, too much ambition and boasting can lead to an overly competitive environment and a perception that you are arrogant. Arrogance is a fatal characteristic in a potential leader. Others are less likely to approach you and want to work with you if you are arrogant. Bragging about the experiences, education, and credentials that you possess could intimidate others or add to the perceived arrogance. Ask the question, "Am I the type of person I would want to be around if given a choice?"

The quality of relationships and your leadership will be most clear when you have made a mistake or erred. If you have been self-serving, arrogant, or insensitive to others, you can expect them to rejoice in your sorrows. If, on the other hand, you've been humble, served others, and have developed a lot of goodwill, your colleagues and friends will come to your rescue and go the extra mile to help you.

Strategies for Being Humble

You are much more likely to have individuals approach you and enjoy working with you if you have a lower-key or humble attitude. An effective strategy is to focus on doing excellent work and optimizing your contribution to the team. Honor, recognition, and appreciation come from others; that is their choice, not yours. The more you seek it, the less you will get. Focus on servant leadership, in an authentic and altruistic manner.

When looking at the results that have been achieved, downplay your accomplishments and focus the appreciation on the team. The confident leader is not concerned with credit. Achieving results is the only barometer, not glory. The lower the profile you take, the more the team may appreciate your efforts as a team leader.

Be helpful to others, without seeking recognition or rewards. Be truly altruistic and supportive of others. Glory seekers are not likely to get into or stay in top leadership. Speak up when it helps the team. When you are done speaking up, go back to learning more so you can contribute more.

Frustration and Anger

It is completely understandable that there will be frustrating moments during your career. There are many possible causes for frustration in the workplace: malfunctioning technology, decisions by leadership, delays, and lack of cooperation, as well as poor personal decisions or lack of skills or knowledge. Frustration can lead to other negative emotions, including anger.

Although it's natural for frustration to develop, it is not productive to show it or let it grow into anger. While there may be a cathartic benefit of releasing some emotion, displaying too much will be damaging. Displaying frustration is usually not going to change anything. It is a reactive, emotional response, like having an adult temper-tantrum, which can be viewed as a sign of immaturity or an ineffective leader. These emotions can make complex problems much more difficult, making it harder to find solutions to issues or to engage others. Dialogue and decisions become driven by negative emotions rather than logic, learning, and experience.

Frustration and anger can interfere with good working relationships. Rather than focusing on the issue or problem, others may try to address your frustration or, worse yet, not want to engage or help you. Colleagues may change their interaction with you out of fear that they will generate or receive more of your frustration. This change diverts focus from the project at hand and could suffocate honest, more productive interactions.

Allowing frustration and anger to show can also be seen by others as an excuse to display their own negative emotions, which could inhibit their effectiveness. This reaction will further limit the ability of a team to interact and work in a productive manner.

Becoming frustrated can also be a career derailer. If you are assigned a complex project, it is because someone believes you have the leadership competency to overcome potential issues and challenges. Showing frustration could be seen as an inability to deal with the challenges. In the future, others could be given similar projects with the assumption that you would not get it done. An effective leader will methodically address each of the roadblocks or speed bumps that appear.

Strategies for Controlling Frustration and Anger

Sample Journal Entry

June 6: One of my strategies to develop over time will be having expert development of my emotional intelligence. Specifically, anger, defensiveness, anxiety, and frustration are emotions that need to be controlled to get the job done. Also, while my passion and enthusiasm can be very positive, too much passion can be very negative.

Rather than displaying frustration, anger, and other negative emotions, many strategies are available for controlling the emotions. The best strategy will depend on the situation.

Identify the Source

The first step is to correctly identify the source of the frustration. There may have been a final tipping point that caused the negative emotion, but you need to identify any underlying causes. Someone once told me that there are two things not to become frustrated or worried about: those things you can't change and those that you can. For those that you can't change...accept reality. For those that you can change...change them.

To identify the source of the emotion, step away from it and calm down. Look back at the situation and analyze it. Ask the following questions:

- What is the cause?
- What went wrong?
- What were my expectations?
- Am I at fault or is someone else?

- What can I do to overcome the issue?
- How do I proceed from here?

Once the true cause is identified, it is possible to control the emotion and proceed in a productive, less emotional manner. For example, frustration can be a result of lack of information. Take a step back and determine what additional information is needed. It may be necessary to ask others for more information or wait until all necessary facts, figures, and decisions are in place before moving forward.

Personal Tactics

Frustration can be a by-product of being "stuck" or spending too much time on a problem. While the intensity or focus on an issue can be helpful, too much can result in stalled or dead-end thinking. Taking a break or working on something else for a while can lessen the frustration. Stepping away allows the mind to shift focus, relax, and look at the same issue in a new way. Einstein once observed that when he went to bed with a problem, he could wake up with the solution waiting for him.

Changing position can also provide a new perspective leading to a new solution around the frustration. I was once advised to stand on a chair or move around to the other side of the desk for a new vantage point. Looking at the issue from another's viewpoint or switching sides or roles with team members can bring about a similar benefit.

Writing in your leadership journal about the source or cause of the frustration can be helpful in managing your emotions. The process of recording the event will lead to a learning opportunity if carried through to identifying solutions or other ways of reacting to the challenge.

Channel the frustration to productive, positive means rather than negative outpourings. Practice patience and control over your negative emotions. Convert the potential negative to a positive response. Let the emotion provide new energy for tackling the challenge. Use humor, a joke, or laughter to brighten the situation and break the negative emotion.

For example, you might start complaining as a solution to handle frustrations. However, the energy to complain (and it does

take energy) will be more effective if channeled to provide positive feedback to improve the situation or eliminate the stressor.
Be aware of how you come across and present the feedback, or it
could still be seen as complaining or blaming. Be mindful of the
reaction to your feedback to ensure it was received in the positive manner that you intended.

A personal lack of knowledge or skills could be the source of the
frustration. Use this as a learning opportunity. Utilize your experiences, resources, and network of colleagues to help you gain
the needed knowledge and work through the situation. There is
usually a toolbox available to help solve a point of frustration.

Successful leaders know that frustration comes with the job; that
there will always be some delay or glitch or change of decision.
One solution is to prepare before issues appear. Develop the
means of identifying potential challenges and have an array
of strategies, resources, and relationships in place to identify
options and design solutions. You and your organization can
develop change management techniques to navigate the potential roadblocks.

Working with Others

Be particularly aware when you sense frustration developing that
you don't display it and allow it to spread to others. Negative
emotions can be contagious and interfere with group interaction
and productivity. Find ways to cut it off or divert emotions if you
sense frustration and negativity building in yourself and your
team.

When you're handling a frustrating situation, it is important to
recognize that others may also be frustrated. This is an opportunity to develop your skills in helping others deal with negative
emotions. Use humor, listening skills, and compassion to deflect
negative emotions and introduce a positive reaction. This can
open up opportunities for joint problem solving.

If others do not share the frustration, then step back and determine the cause of your frustration. Is there an adequate reason
for it or is it just another bump in the road? You may view your
frustration as the result of others' actions, but it may have been
your fault. Did you adequately explain the results you expected
or the timeline? Did you assign a task to the appropriate person

EXHIBIT 1.3 ■ Advice for Controlling Frustration and Anger

Advice	Opportunity for Change
Don't let yourself wallow in the current situation and engage in negative emotions and behavior. Don't remain locked in your position if the frustration and anger continue.	Attempt to change the situation or try a different strategy to solve it. If it's a temporary situation, then learn to make the best of it. If your occupation is the problem, consider whether changing jobs is the best strategy.
Don't react in a way that continues or exacerbates the frustration.	Take time to control your emotions and react in a less negative and more positive manner. Consider using humor or accept the event as another of life's experiences and move on.
Don't become agitated when others are angry. Don't become defensive.	Remain calm and control your emotions while waiting for the steam to be released. When everyone has calmed down, express how their anger made you feel. This won't be easy if the angry person was a supervisor, but it may be necessary to maintain a working relationship.
Don't bottle up your anger (for an eventual blowup).	Instead, channel the anger into respectful dialogue, discussion, debate, and decisions – the four "Ds" – in order to avoid the last D: divisiveness.
Don't overreact when mistakes are made; oftentimes it is the reaction to the event (denial, cover-up, anger, etc.) that cause severe damage.	Everyone makes mistakes, but it is how we react that will determine the next sequence of events. Forgiveness and learning from the mistake are positive ways to react.

with the appropriate skills? Did you have unrealistic expectations? Is there an opportunity for development or coaching to raise the skills and confidence of a team member?

During times of frustration and high emotion, it is easy to say words that can damage relationships. Saying something out of frustration does not minimize the damage that is caused or the hurt inflicted; it merely provides an excuse for why it was said. This is when relationships can be damaged. Be mindful of the effect of your emotions on others. Exhibit 1.3 offers recommendations for managing your frustration and anger.

Anxiety

Anxiety is natural, given the magnitude of problems and challenges leaders face. It arises from uncertainty, ambiguity, new challenges, and fear. In a world of rapid change, the "permanent whitewater" of our environment, the opportunity for anxiety to develop, is always present. Organizational sources of anxiety can include unclear goals, confusing priorities, the lack of clarity by team members, inadequate resources, the timing of initiatives, a preoccupation with other issues that may be able to wait, or improper delegation.

Unfortunately, anxiety is a nonproductive emotional interference. It can be extremely damaging if it drains energy that could be used to solve problems or if it raises an emotional veil that reduces the ability to find creative solutions. Anxiety can impact self-confidence and self-esteem, creating further anxiety and resulting in a continuing escalation of negative emotions.

Anxiety can also lead to the perception by others that you are not confident or are timid, which can reduce their confidence in you. To hide anxiety, you might develop a defensiveness or arrogance, both of which will negatively impact relationships. Others may not approach you or they may be hesitant to work closely with you.

If uncertainty, ambiguity, chaos, and volatility are here to stay, then stress and anxiety should be expected. To not feel them might be a result of underestimating the magnitude of an issue. How you choose to respond to the emotions can be both healthy and unhealthy. It can be unhealthy if you are affected so much that physical or emotional ailments begin to develop. However, anxiety and stress can also provide the motivation to learn, work harder, and develop some different strategy that might not otherwise have been contemplated. A little bit of stress can be beneficial, but a lot can be damaging. The secret is in controlling your emotions.

Today's rapidly changing business world is similar to the environment that special operations forces in the military operate in. They are expected to react instantly to changing conditions and create options and strategies with emerging information. Through repeated training and learning, they develop the skills to control their negative emotions and gain the confidence to know their decisions and adjustments to changing conditions will win over the situation. These are the skills and knowledge that you will need to learn and develop with time and practice.

Strategies for Managing Anxiety

I was inspired by a particular concept in the book *Man's Search for Meaning* by Victor Frankl (2000), that there is an ultimate freedom we all have that can't be taken away: the freedom of choice on how we respond to circumstances. This concept is empowering, as it eliminates the excuse of something or someone else making me feel or react in a certain way. It is up to me to allow anxiety to occur or not.

One of the many examples of anxiety in my career involved my enrollment in the doctoral program in organization development. During the first few days of the week-long introductory course, what started out as enthusiastic zeal turned into complete overload and anxiety. Memories of failures in elementary and high school were penetrating my thoughts, reminding me of my weaknesses in research and writing. The overarching thought was "how will I ever complete this program and a dissertation?" A good night's sleep on the fourth day led to a new morning and the beginning of a "new me." I journalized strategies on how I would rearrange my daily routine, redistribute priorities, and focus my efforts. I knew the goal of receiving the doctor of education degree would be achieved one assignment and one class at a time.

You can apply several of these same strategies in overcoming anxiety. Step back and reflect on the cause leading to the emotions. Identify the environmental factors that are allowing the anxiety to grow. What are your expectations? Transform the anxiety into focused attention to resolve the issue(s). Identify how your emotions and reaction can be redirected to derive a positive benefit. Anxiety may also be your intuition saying "caution, proceed with care." You may need to slow down a bit to assess what is going on before proceeding too rapidly.

Use your leadership journal to write down the anxiety and the source of it. Recording the effect will provide some cathartic benefit. Then sort through what can be done to mitigate the source. Take the position that all issues can be resolved if the proper strategies can be developed. Treat it like a puzzle rather than a mystery. Puzzles can be solved, whereas mysteries may not be. Be creative when looking at the issues causing the anxiety and trying to identify solutions. Understand that others may have some of the puzzle pieces – you are not in this alone.

While some initial anxiety is natural and an honest emotion, ruminating or continuous and obsessive worrying is wasteful to achieving excellence. Channeling as much energy as possible to positive actions will be more effective than worrying. Think through the vision and the ideal end result. Develop strategies and initiatives to achieve the progress necessary to move toward the vision. Let an optimistic orientation drive the progress toward the desired end state.

New tasks and assignments can result in substantial anxiety. Don't let it create a vicious cycle of underperformance through procrastination, rumination, and worry. Look upon new tasks as a challenge you will master, a fun new puzzle, or an opportunity to add to your leadership toolbox. Break up complex projects into pieces or sections. Seek advice, add new team members, incorporate new information, and consider new alternatives. Let persistence and resolve carry you through.

Anxiety can develop if you think you don't have the needed skill or knowledge and will look incompetent or foolish. It is much more likely that you know as much as others do, but the problem has not been vetted and others are asking you to resolve it. There is no need to have an answer on the first day. Allow time to learn and reflect on how to proceed. Assemble a team of colleagues who have different insights into the issue. Identify the questions that when answered will provide a comprehensive framework to resolve the issue. Apply the process of how doctoral dissertations are accomplished: start with a problem or a research question, gather information (a literature review), develop a methodology, identify results, and discuss what was learned. While most problems don't require an entire doctoral dissertation process, the approach can be very helpful in framing issues.

Another source of anxiety is poor planning. Inadequate planning leads to poor assessment, strategizing, and implementation. Knowing that you are "rushing through" something creates anxiety – you know that this is not the way to do something. Others who are impacted will notice the lack of preparation and poor implementation. Communication will likely suffer. Accordingly, stepping back to reflect on the process and considering corrections will provide an opportunity to overcome the poor planning and reduce the anxiety.

Fear of not doing the right thing can cause you to delay making decisions or proceeding until you are absolutely certain of the correct path. However, you may be waiting for utopia, an ideal place that does not exist. Waiting too long will be seen as overly cautious and timid and could result in missed opportunities, especially in a dynamic environment. Yes, at times a wait-and-see approach may be the best strategy. However, rather than waiting, you may need a different tactic:

- Identify a decision or prepare a plan with the best available knowledge;
- Identify potential obstacles or unforeseen circumstances;
- Develop alternative actions to adapt to new information and changing circumstances; and
- Implement the decision or the plan.

This is where the adaptable, practical, resourceful leader can demonstrate high value by assertively implementing strategies in uncertain times.

When you are feeling anxious, overwhelmed, frustrated, and stressed out, look around and see if everyone else is feeling the same or worse. Then use your leadership skills (analytical, interpersonal, strategic, business, etc.) to think through how you can help yourself and others. Your reputation and credibility as a leader will emerge. Your responses under stress will be noticed by others. This is when leaders are made.

EXHIBIT 1.4 ■ Advice for Managing Anxiety

Advice	Opportunity for Change
Don't display anxiety.	Acknowledge your anxiety. Learn to address anxiety assertively through diverting the energy to positive reactions.
Don't let anxiety result in blaming, shaming, complaining, and being irritable or frustrated with others.	Take the time to control your emotions and reflect on the causes and solutions for issues.
Don't waste time rehashing or obsessing the same points over and over again, or thinking too much about something.	Learn from past actions, including mistakes, and move on.
Don't deal with anxiety by working harder or longer, skipping exercising, overeating, drinking too much alcohol, smoking, or taking drugs.	Maintain a healthy lifestyle and manage stress or anxiety by taking a break, exercising regularly, talking with others, etc.
Don't let doubts cause excessive anxiety or worry.	Let doubts encourage you to take a critical look at issues, to reflect, and to obtain more information.
Don't wait to make decisions until there are conditions of certainty and no anxiety.	Gather a reasonable amount of information, make decisions with the best available information, and prepare to adjust as necessary.

Organizational anxiety is going to occur during times of stress, especially financial stress, as individuals may perceive that jobs are at stake. This is when a calm, assertive presence will be very helpful. This reaction may help reduce anxiety in others and increase their confidence in your leadership skills. They may be more likely to develop and share ideas to help resolve the issues. Exhibit 1.4 lists suggestions for managing anxiety.

Optimism

Optimism, the belief that all will be okay, is very powerful. Spiritual and religious traditions encourage faith and optimism. Leaders need optimism that the knowledge, resources, relationships, and resiliency that they've developed will enable them to conquer challenges and achieve desired goals. Being optimistic can channel your attention to those choices more likely to result in the desired outcomes.

Every career has ups and downs, successes and disappointments. You can deal with the setbacks by considering that "there was a reason this happened." This optimistic orientation can become a self-fulfilling prophecy because you will work energetically toward finding a more compatible new goal or vision. Avoid any negativity that may try to find roots during these sensitive times. I was once told to fertilize and nurture the grass and flowers, not the weeds.

Leaders need to be optimistic and higher-level leaders even more. Midlevel managers and staff are going to be profoundly impacted by the optimism (or lack of it) that leaders show. The optimism (or pessimism) will spread very rapidly, so be mindful of how you are perceived by others. Followers are attracted by sincere and realistic hope or optimism. You need to be honest about the realities of the situation, but it will be the optimism that will carry the message and influence efforts of change.

Strategies for Developing Optimism

Optimism is part of our personality, but it can also be developed or displayed in a variety of ways. The most appropriate path toward optimism will depend on your personality and circumstances, or you can use a combination of methods. Some strategies include:

- Being physically fit;
- Being enthusiastic;
- Knowing and living your values;
- Maintaining a high energy level;
- Having a positive attitude; and
- Always learning new skills and acquiring knowledge.

Optimism is one of the choices available to you when faced with challenges or goals. There are other choices, such as worrying and negative self-talk. Optimism must prevail over worry, as this nonoptimistic reaction is not productive at nurturing relationships and strategies to achieve the goals. Precious time and energy will be lost, forever. Be mindful of negative thoughts and replace them with self-coaching and mentoring through reflection and other learning strategies.

Big disappointments or changes, like losing a job or becoming divorced, can be enormous opportunities to rethink, repriori- tize, and restrategize. Before the event, you might not have been looking for a change. Now, you have an opportunity, even if it's forced upon you, to create a new future. This requires optimism or faith that the new future will turn out well. Approach these opportunities with optimism to reevaluate your life and career, to create a new and better future than what previously existed.

Let optimism and being positive crowd out the negative thoughts, providing more of an opportunity to identify and implement strategies that will lead to desired results. Think of all barriers as new challenges. Assume that you can handle them or move around them to continue moving toward the goal.

Negative self-talk can be an obstacle to success. The conversa- tions with yourself and others need to paint an inspiring future of what you want to achieve. Identify the strategies that will improve performance. Keep the image in mind of the desired end state and strive toward that positive end. Being positive may also reduce stress or other negative responses, diverting the expenditure of energy from negative to positive reactions.

Optimism is also a potent adversary to negative reactions from others. It is natural for others to resist change or have other rea- sons for undesirable responses. This response can be presented as anger, frustration, criticism, or aggressive behaviors. As a leader you can react defensively or take the response personally. Or you can be sensitive to the reasons behind the negative behaviors of others. Share your optimism that the chosen direction is correct and let it persuade others to join in. Being optimistic will facili- tate engaging followers.

Learn to recognize when it's time to face reality. For example, don't let optimism lead you to overestimate your competencies or someone else's. Recognize and accept the evidence that the knowledge and skills to complete a task may be lacking, and that new training or a new person may be needed. Realize when a task or goal is impossible and needs to be changed. Exhibit 1.5 lists more advice for developing optimism.

EXHIBIT 1.5 ■ Advice for Developing Optimism

Advice	Opportunity for Change
Don't be guided by your fears or apprehension, either of which may become a self-fulfilling prophecy.	Let optimism and a positive attitude be your guide.
Don't let your optimism blind you to reality. Too much optimism can be a fault. Don't think optimism will make the unbelievable or unattainable possible.	Know when to accept reality.
Limit the amount of "over the top" optimism or emotions; otherwise, you may create a lack of credibility.	Moderate your emotions to what's appropriate for you and your setting. Share your optimism, but have the data and resources to back it up

Patience

Being patient is a critical leadership skill. It is necessary to control impatience like controlling frustration, anger, and anxiety in yourself and others. These are strong emotions that can generate a negative cascading of more emotions and reactions. Patience is needed when working with others and to address disappointments or failures on your part or by others.

Patience is also necessary to allow time for the development of strategies when facing very complex projects or during times of uncertainty. Patience is required when decisions or priorities seem to be constantly changing, generating wasted effort and frustration. These types of situations describe a large portion of work life. It is unlikely you can succeed in your career or leadership without patience.

Being patient is effectively being respectful to others, giving them the benefit of the doubt, going the extra mile to learn what is going on. Being patient with others will:

- Allow relationships to be developed and maintained;
- Provide time for solutions to emerge;
- Encourage others to also be patient; and
- Demonstrate the acceptance that everyone is human; delays and mistakes happen.

Strategies for Practicing Patience

When encountering feelings of frustration, a successful strategy is to practice patience. Frustration can be the result of not knowing what to do, facing unexpected and unwanted obstacles, or having new environmental factors set you back. Because frustration can lead to stronger negative reactions (and can damage self-esteem and relationships), patience is a highly effective alternative and an opportunity to improve leadership effectiveness.

For example, rather than getting frustrated or stressed as a result of something you had no role in or ability to influence, practice patience. Demonstrating patience under these circumstances does not mean that you accept what has happened as being right or justified, but that you recognize that bad things do happen. Use it as a learning opportunity for yourself and others involved and don't dwell on it.

Allow patience and time to build relationships with others. Even the most competent individual needs to allow others the time and opportunity to evaluate your competencies and personality.

Patience is going to be tested under conditions of uncertainty. For example, uncertainty is huge when starting a new job. If it's a new job in a new industry in a new city, you will likely experience major stress. This is when it is particularly important to take the time to settle in and learn. While there is a natural desire to jump in and contribute, it may be better to be patient with transitions. Allow for a period of adjustment and learning about the job and others expectations of you.

The most significant test of my patience was when I accepted a huge promotion in another community. I went from a midlevel manager in a large, well-established medical group practice with enormous resources to my new position as the chief administrative officer in a newly formed practice. I essentially went from middle management to the top without the benefit of a gradual transition, nor did I have experience in most of the functions of this new role. Patience was one of the crucial attributes that carried me through the assimilation and integration into this situation, while learning as quickly as possible.

Complex assignments or issues require adequate time for solutions to be identified and implemented, and the results tracked and understood. There is a pacing to progress that sometimes is slow and painful. To not anticipate or appreciate this fact is naïve. That does not mean that you shouldn't hold yourself or others accountable to timetables. If you proactively identify the amount of time needed before making any judgments about the assignment, you will reduce the likelihood of becoming frustrated or impatient. Don't rush into premature decisions or conclusions; allow time for deciding on and implementing the correct solution and wait for the results to develop.

A true leader must also balance the fine line between patience and accountability. Individuals need to be held accountable to their responsibilities, timelines, and relationships with others. Leaders need to recognize when patience will be rewarded with success and when others are not being accountable for their actions or are not capable of completing their tasks. When the latter is the case, no amount of patience will resolve the issue.

Being patient with others is especially important when they are learning new skills, tackling new tasks, or going through difficult times. When passing through transitions, realize that others may not accept new ideas or changes as quickly as you do. Allow them time to adjust and to "see" what you have been suggesting. Give others the time to adapt, cognitively and emotionally. Take the time to listen to their stories, be empathetic, and understand their reasons for hesitancy.

Developing patience is an important strategy to deal with the inevitable delays in highly bureaucratic or complex organizations. Change involves risk by the decision makers. Also, change will be more effective with support by leadership. Be patient and accepting that leaders need to work through the issues and the process before implementing change. When I get frustrated with delays in starting a project or new initiative, I remember being told of a bamboo tree that for the first four years grows very little, but during the fifth year it can grow 80 feet. During those first four years, the roots are growing deep and the plant is developing the structure needed to succeed. If you allow time for the roots to develop in your business, you may be amazed at the results that follow.

EXHIBIT 1.6 ■ Advice for Practicing Patience

Advice	Opportunity for Change
Don't overreact to circumstances.	Let patience help you control your emotions and react appropriately to the circumstances.
Don't let impatience take over when progress is not being made or when you are disappointed with yourself or others.	Do practice patience, along with being positive and persistent. Anyone can excel when everything is going the right way. Leaders shine in how they deal with roadblocks and disasters.
Don't get irritated when decisions or changes are delayed.	Understand that it takes time to ensure the correct decisions are made and changes can be correctly implemented.

You can also practice patience in understanding the reasons why particular decisions are made. Some are explicit reasons (policies, procedures, etc.), but others are not described formally. The latter decisions are made for cultural or historical reasons. Cultures are conservative in nature and are resistant to change, especially changes introduced by someone new to the unit or organization. It is important to learn the culture and history to understand how change is accomplished within the organization. Be patient and your influence may be rewarded. This is an application of the Prayer of St. Francis and one of Steven Covey's (1989) habits in the book, *The 7 Habits of Highly Effective People*: "seek first to understand, then to be understood."

Exhibit 1.6 offers more advice for practicing patience.

Resilience

While we all wish that life would only have "ups," we all know that there are also valleys, the down times in life. This can happen with short-term, temporary conditions (delays or overly challenging assignments) or longer-term situations such as working under a difficult boss or realizing you have taken the wrong job. To handle these valleys, individuals need to have resilience. Many of the strategies outlined in other chapters can be very helpful in these times, but the foundation for those approaches is having a resilient personality.

Resilience is defined as:

- The ability to recover quickly from illness, change, or misfortune; or
- The property of a material that enables it to resume its original shape or position after being bent, stretched, or compressed; elasticity (*American Heritage Dictionary* 2009).

You can demonstrate resilience and professionalism by managing how you react to and recover from setbacks in work and life. Maintaining a level of dedication and enthusiasm despite the routine, boredom, or difficulty of a job or task will also demonstrate resilience. Rise to the occasion by identifying new ways of accomplishing tasks or addressing poor results and continuously performing at your best to achieve world-class results.

Your resilience when faced with difficult situations will be among the leadership traits that will be evaluated by others. This is why behaviorally based interview questions are increasingly used for candidates, to assess how you have actually acted in a variety of difficult situations. Developing resilience now will enable you to demonstrate leadership qualities to carry you forward in new situations and positions.

Strategies for Developing Resilience

Strategies for developing resilience include:

- Adapt to the circumstances at hand and thrive under them;
- Accept setbacks;
- Accept change that you can't control; don't resist it;
- Determine what you can change in yourself and your environment and then change it;
- Let go of things or habits that are no longer working; and
- Change your reactions to others to improve relationships and results.

During times of disappointment or failure, take the time to reflect, assess, learn, and move on. The learning individual and organization will have the resilience to turn these challenges into a learning opportunity and to achieve a higher "return" on what was learned. When faced with disappointment, you can naturally feel many negative emotions. Rather than let these emotions be overwhelming, you can choose to take the other road: don't overreact; continue to perform outstanding work, be optimistic, take the time to develop skills or competencies you don't have, and reflect on your priorities and values.

No matter how things appear to be going, keep moving forward with optimism that the goals will be achieved. Pessimism is a negative influencer. It breeds more pessimism and can be self-fulfilling. If you need assistance, ask for it. Work through the situation with the eyes of a student; this is an opportunity to learn a lesson. This resilience can be positive.

There is a phrase in the military that "no plan survives the first contact with the enemy." This advice is helpful to avoid being wedded to strategies that were developed. An ability to learn and adjust is important for leaders in the various circumstances they find themselves in. While the mission and vision are constant and clear, the strategies may need to be adapted or changed as needed. Anticipate what may require a change and build-in the ability to adjust.

Remember the phrase "sometimes things happen for a reason." For example, when you do not receive a promotion, disappointment is natural in the short term but will be damaging if allowed to persist. In this example, the reason for not receiving the promotion might be that others realized it was not a good match for you. A sign of resilience under such circumstances is to reflect and do some soul searching rather than holding on to the disappointment. Then you may be in a better position to seek other opportunities that may be a better fit or otherwise would have been ignored. Look at a disappointment as an opportunity to learn something new, try a different approach, or develop some complementary skills that will achieve positive results the next time. This may be an opportunity to recreate yourself – to start a new career or path that you've always wondered about.

When stress or frustration seems overwhelming, being mindfully resilient will help see you through. That is, recognize the stress and plan how you will work yourself out of it. There is no need to deny the stress, as this is not recognizing reality; having a plan to bounce back is what is critical.

Taking on leadership roles can result in massive criticism and negativity being directed at you. Over time, this can wear you down. To develop and maintain resiliency requires self-esteem (without becoming insensitive or arrogant) and perseverance. Accept and learn from the criticism if it is deserved – if, for example, your decision was inappropriate or you set unrealistic expectations. For undeserved criticism, try not to personalize it, but look for the reason behind it and identify an appropriate, controlled response. Also, let your resilience help you focus on what has been accomplished and celebrate the incremental gains that move the organization in the right direction.

Part of maintaining resilience is having a healthy work–life balance and integration for now and the future. Pacing yourself is important, otherwise you run the risk that you will run out of "gas" or be unable to spring back from disappointments. The work–life balance is what provides the energy storehouse to regroup and develop new strategies so that you are starting from a position of strength. Trying to rebound when you are exhausted is going to be much more challenging. Remember to eat well, exercise regularly, and get enough sleep; take time for enjoyment to refresh yourself; and surround yourself with positive people.

One of the great stories of resilience led to the concept of the "Stockdale Paradox," the combination of accepting the brutal reality of the situation with a faith that you will eventually prevail. This paradox was identified as an attribute of successful leaders and organizations described by Jim Collins in his book *Good to Great: Why Some Companies Make the Leap...and Others Don't* (2001). James Stockdale was a high-ranking naval officer who was captured during the Vietnam War. He was held at the "Hanoi Hilton" prison for eight years, tortured, with no reason for hope or sense of control, and yet he became stronger during capture. He didn't let himself become depressed or lose faith, and he decided to turn the experience into the defining event of his life, to make himself stronger. He felt that he survived better than the optimists because they had short-term goals, potential dates for their releases, that were not fulfilled, and they couldn't handle the repeated disappointments. The Stockdale Paradox says, "You must maintain unwavering faith that you can and will prevail in the end, regardless of the difficulties, *AND at the*

EXHIBIT 1.7 ■ Advice for Developing Resilience

Advice	Opportunity for Change
Don't dwell on disappointments or setbacks.	Anticipate that there will be failures or "wrong turns." Conduct an "after action review" and apply the lessons learned to future cases.
Don't become defensive during setbacks or at critical times. Becoming defensive will minimize learning, fracture relationships, and may result in loss of your job.	Accept responsibility, if appropriate, and respond with controlled emotions. Acknowledge these times as learning opportunities.
Don't complain or turn down bad assignments, even if they seem like "suicide missions."	Accept these assignments as valuable learning opportunities and as tests of your abilities and commitment. Not all seeds bear fruit, but that does not mean you don't keep planting.
Don't get stuck in resistance.	Accept change.

same time have the discipline to confront the most brutal facts of your current reality, whatever they might be" (Collins 2001). Exhibit 1.7 offers recommendations for developing resilience.

Confidence

Confidence is a result of experience and having a track record for achieving results and solving difficult challenges. This comes with time and experience; it can't be forced. Confidence without experience is helpful in avoiding needless anxiety, but confidence with experience is more powerful, much like facts are more helpful than opinions. Experience adds credibility to approaches so that prior learning can be integrated into current strategies. Over time, experience is gained, which generates more confidence.

Leaders are constantly confronted with new problems and situations. Confidence is knowing that this is part of the position. Even if you don't have an immediate answer, you will be able to find an answer and develop a solution based on new knowledge and past experience. Confidence is more likely to develop when you recognize that at times life is absurd but there will always be a way to deal with it.

Achieving excellence requires confidence. Without confidence, you are not likely to risk making changes, create higher expectations, or persist in the face of adversity. Confidence is a necessary building block. Confidence is self-efficacy, the belief that you can do the job.

A lack of confidence can result in many negative effects: paralysis in making decisions, inhibition in learning new tasks, and less likelihood of taking on risks out of fear of failure. Poor self-confidence can result in health issues, in lower satisfaction, and ultimately may lead to a self-fulfilling prophecy of reduced success in relationships and tasks.

Confidence has a direct relationship to leadership effectiveness. If you do not have the confidence that you can accomplish something, there is a greater likelihood that you will not even attempt it. You won't explore new opportunities, learn new capabilities, or utilize your talent. Although it is desirable to have a sense of humility or humbleness, you also need to have self-efficacy or belief in yourself.

Strategies for Developing Confidence

You can develop confidence by reflecting on past accomplishments and successes to identify and categorize strategies that have worked well in the past. Self-confidence is gained with a reflection of your strengths and weaknesses. Think about conducting a SWOT (strengths, weaknesses, opportunities, threats) analysis to identify your internal strengths and weaknesses. Recognize the external opportunities and threats and how you will overcome them. Confidence can be a "self-fulfilling prophecy," because it will likely carry you through to success.

Being confident does not mean that you have the answers. It is the confidence that you will discover the answers through process, inquiry, and teamwork. Yes, there is ambiguity and uncertainty; this is part of the process.

Having some self-doubt is natural when new to a role or when dealing with complex projects. An appropriate amount of self-doubt can be helpful, but be careful that it does not become disabling. Use this emotion or humility to energize you toward gaining needed knowledge and to identify solutions to the challenges. Also, reflect on prior solutions and successes that can provide helpful ideas to be utilized with the new situation. These prior experiences will provide a foundation to overcoming the new challenges. You won't need to start from scratch.

It is quite natural to feel despondent when something does not go well, but don't let it shake your confidence. This could lead to insecurity and to underperformance, creating a further loss of confidence. Instead of getting caught up in negative thoughts, recognize that no one succeeds all the time. Reframe the less-than-desirable outcome from being a "failure" to one of a "lesson" and identify what can be learned. Think about it as a physicist might: you took some actions, you got some results. If you want different results, take different actions.

I remember an incident when I was suddenly and unexpectedly informed that I would be assigned to another specialty in the medical group practice. I could have let this shake my confidence or taken it personally and defensively. Instead, I recognized that, from time to time, a "chemistry" in relationships with others may not be productive and it is appropriate to seek a new position. I accepted the transition with confidence and my new role was a much better fit, given my talents and the personalities of the individuals involved.

Have the confidence to break free of situations and processes that you are comfortable with. Although there is a feeling of security and comfort staying with the tried and true, it can be very dangerous if you become complacent. We need new assignments and tasks to learn new approaches and gain from new experiences. This is where innovation comes from: the blending of new ideas with current or future problems. Yes, at first you will feel uncomfortable, potentially even incompetent, while tackling a new situation, but let your confidence carry you through. Recognize that this will be a temporary period in the necessary process of change.

When having and displaying a calm sense of confidence, others will be more likely to become comfortable with your ideas than if you are agitated. Your confidence should result in a calmer delivery when dealing with others. This does not mean a lack of assertiveness, just a calmer approach. Confident leaders

EXHIBIT 1.8 ■ Advice for Developing Confidence

Advice	Opportunity for Change
Don't lose confidence when results are not favorable.	Let your ability to be resilient, to learn, and to accept the undesirable results carry you with professional poise, knowing that this is a building block for the future.
Don't think you must have all the answers all the time.	Have the confidence that you will gain the knowledge to develop a process or approach to resolve the issue.
Don't be afraid to ask others for opinions or help.	No one has all the answers. Surround yourself with team members who have complementary knowledge and know when to seek their input.
Don't display lack of confidence.	Others may start to become anxious or panic if they perceive a lack of confidence. Remain calm and try to pacify those around you.
Don't accept the status quo out of fear of the new and unknown.	Have the confidence to accept new challenges and try new approaches.
Don't think your confidence will keep you from making mistakes.	Mistakes will occur and leaders will err. Reflect on your decisions and actions to identify potential mistakes or alternative actions. Learn from them.

recognize that "losing it" will only be counterproductive, wasting energy and time, and possibly damaging relationships.

There will be individuals who don't support your ideas, don't like you, or don't have confidence in you. Some individuals may even want you to fail. Remember, for every new idea or innovation, there will be individuals offering resistance and fighting for the status quo, either out of jealousy, fear, greed, or other reasons. To handle these situations, you will need a delicate balance between being sensitive and having a "thick skin." The thick skin is the resilience and confidence to help you deal with their negativity and resistance. Over time, you will develop the knowledge of strategies that do and don't work, both in human relations management and business strategies. Have the confidence that you are doing the best you can using all of your talents. Focus on continuous improvement, inspiring others to follow you. This is one of the many challenges of leadership.

EXHIBIT 1.9 ■ Questions for Reflection: Leading Self

Learning:	What learning strategies are key to your success? How do you maintain an open mind to new ideas?
Reflection:	How do you build in reflection time to keep a focus on the vision? Do you have a special place or sanctuary that facilitates reflection?
Humility:	Do you think others perceive you as being humble? What strategies do you use to avoid displaying arrogance?
Frustration and Anger:	How do you address frustrating situations? What strategies do you employ to minimize anger?
Anxiety:	When faced with highly sensitive challenges, how do you control anxiety? When your colleagues are overly anxious, how do you help them deal with the situation?
Optimism:	When faced with challenging circumstances, how do you evoke optimism? How do you balance optimism with a realistic assessment of the future?
Patience:	How do you balance patience with accountability? What strategies do you deploy to have patience with others?
Resilience:	What strategies do you use to deal with failures? How successful are you in adjusting to extreme levels of stress?
Confidence:	How do you achieve a healthy balance of skepticism with confidence? Do you maintain confidence when things don't go well? How do you coach team members who lack confidence?

Action Items: What two or three specific actions will you commit to as a result of reading this chapter on Leading Self through Learning?

1. _____

2. _____

3. _____

Positions with more responsibility are going to take more "shots." This is the nature of top management because there are normally very few individuals in those positions and it is easy to point blame. Leaders in these positions need a higher level of confidence and the ability to never take attacks personally. While attacks can be personal, most of the time they are more a verbal sharing of frustration, anger, or other emotional reactions. Being confident will generate a more positive response. Exhibit 1.8 lists suggestions for developing confidence.

Conclusion

There is a lot to think about, learn, and practice related to leading oneself. It is important to remember these topics to learn more about yourself and how to develop your leadership capabilities. Pause occasionally to reflect on what has been learned and identify what needs to be improved and/or practiced. The questions for reflection in Exhibit 1.9 may be helpful to consider on each of the topics related to leading oneself.

CHAPTER TWO

Leading Others by Developing Relationships

Integrated Leadership Model

**Leading Others:
Developing Relationships**

- Professionalism
- Listening
- Conflict
- Assertiveness
- Diversity and Inclusiveness
- Perspective

**Leading Self:
Through Learning**

- Reflection
- Humility
- Frustration, Anger, Anxiety
- Optimism and Patience
- Resilience and Confidence

**Work-Life
Integration
and
Synergy**

**Leading Organizations:
Achieving Excellence**

- Vision
- Priorities and Being Organized
- Initiative
- Problem Solving
- Change Management
- Achieving Results

©2013 Ronald Menaker

Relationships

Most of the leadership and organization development books that I have read (listed in the bibliography) emphasize the importance of putting people first. Leaders of many successful companies recognize that it's the human effort, from the frontline staff to the top leadership, that generates results to make the company great. It is all about people development to achieve organizational development.

Also, in today's complex and rapidly changing business and healthcare environment, leaders need more support than ever before. Huge demands are placed on leaders, requiring them to rely on their supporting colleagues and network to understand the changes and to assist in identifying and implementing strategies to be successful. The broader the network, the more advice and knowledge a leader is able to access.

With these two factors in mind, it's becoming increasingly important for leaders to have exceptionally strong people skills. MBA and healthcare administration degrees focus on negotiation, marketing, and finance...all important disciplines. However, the degree programs need more focus on potentially the most difficult skill: relationships with others. Focusing on people first is how you will obtain the results you seek.

Developing good personal and business relationships and having strong interpersonal skills are vital for several reasons, including:

- It fosters the ability to encourage and obtain the best efforts from employees, team members, and colleagues;
- Employees and colleagues want to do their best for the leader they respect, trust, and like;
- It facilitates others to trust and commit to ideas and strategies;
- Having a broad network provides leaders with many mentoring and learning opportunities; and
- The ability to maintain relationships and support carries the leader and the organization through criticism and difficult times.

The concept of learning can be applied to building relationships. There is much to be learned from others and not just on how they tackle the job and the ideas they have for improving the organization. Those around you also have different capabilities in relationship building, as well as interacting with and learning from others, that you can emulate.

How you treat others will determine how successful you will be in developing meaningful relationships. Treating others with respect will result in more respect given to you. Have compassion and concern for others and they will reciprocate. It may not take place immediately but, over the long term, relationships will form and be enhanced. Relationships will be developed by your choice of words and actions. You can decide to be (a) positive, inspiring, optimistic, and enthusiastic, or (b) negative, pessimistic, and indifferent.

Always remember that a leader is a leader because others will voluntarily follow one who leads. If you don't build relationships based on mutual trust and respect, will others have a reason to follow your lead? Reflect on your leadership skills and how you engage your followers. Are you helping others? Do you treat them with respect? Do you want to work for someone like you? Would "you" follow you?

Strategies for Developing Relationships

Sample Journal Entry

April 14: Rotary's motto, "Service Above Self," is something I should contemplate. My success and happiness will be enhanced by giving to others. I will build my relationships and have an enriched life. I have all that I need and almost all of what I want.

When thinking about your leadership skills, decide if you want to be known as a leader for your "power and politics," or because you can get things done AND you have great relationships. In developing relationships with others, successful leaders will:

- Be comfortable with people no matter what title or position they have,
- Seek to learn from others;
- Be authentic and not try to be someone other than themselves;
- Know the importance of listening to others; and
- Appreciate and acknowledge the contributions of others.

Develop the ability to relate comfortably with all people, regardless of position. Being approachable is an important leadership attribute. Relationships will be enhanced if others approach you knowing that helping them will be the focus of your attention. Serve others, listen to them, and show appreciation for their efforts. Relationship enhancement is directly correlated with presence and committing time to others. Coaching, mentoring, and nurturing others will be very helpful in building relationships. In doing so, you communicate the message that you care about them.

Relationships will be impacted by the perception others have of your ability, position, and presence. Think through what affect you may be having on people. Learn to read your audience. Are you generating pleasant or unpleasant feelings? Do you think others see you as being approachable, trusting, helpful, supportive, and encouraging? Being aware of these perceptions will provide information to shape your interactions with others in order to optimize each relationship and the contributions you can make.

When meeting and interacting with others, learn how they approach tasks and challenges. Some may have creative problem-solving skills that result in a high level of performance for themselves and the organization. Listen to their ideas and consider adopting these approaches, factoring in some of the strategies of the best models. Build on your own unique approaches to create an authentic approach to leadership.

Realize that you may need to change your reactions to others in order to improve relationships and results. There will be some individuals whose personalities or work styles don't match your method or expectations. As long as they are accomplishing their responsibilities, it is up to you to deal with your reaction. You probably won't be able to change people and their personalities, but you can adapt how you react to and work with them in order to strengthen the relationships.

Your relationships will become better and your happiness increased when you shift the focus of your work effort to how you can help others. Yes, it is natural to want to benefit; however, helping others may be more satisfying. When you help others achieve results, relationships will be developed. Others need your assistance just like you will need theirs.

It is undesirable to talk about yourself when engaging with others in an attempt to establish your worth and credibility. No one wants to hang around with someone who is only interested in talking about themselves and their accomplishments. When engaging with others, focus on their needs and interests first. Simply keep your attention on helping others sincerely, effectively, consistently, altruistically, and with selflessness and trustworthiness. This type of focus will establish a perception of your leadership trait as directed toward serving others.

Strive to be the go-to person for your leadership and mentoring skills. Make your presence desirable and invaluable because of your high level of contributions, and for your interpersonal and technical skills. You will know that you have excellent relationships when others are advocating for you, when your colleagues want you on their teams. Do not draw attention to yourself; instead, focus on the team and organizational needs.

Showing appreciation and acknowledging the contribution of others has a profound impact on developing relationships. Expressing gratitude shows that you have noticed and appreciated others' efforts and are giving credit to them. This will provide reinforcement for the behavior that was acknowledged and will enhance your relationship. Take the time to frequently thank those that have been helpful to you or the organization. Don't let anyone feel that they are being taken for granted.

Always remember that it is the little things that are really the big things. A thank-you note (handwritten), an impromptu lunch, an acknowledgment of appreciation – these are all important messages that show you care about people. The network of relationships is what will generate the results. People will remember how you made them feel and will want to continue working with you. I remember hearing about a car dealer in the Midwest that built his business empire by having the entire management team write 10 thank-you notes every day of the year.

Giving others the benefit of the doubt will almost always result in a favorable outcome and enhance the relationship. There is usually a good reason why something happened the way it did, including why there were delays. Many times, it is the amount of work being required of individuals, especially as organizations are trying to do more with less. There may not have been clarity with regard to roles and responsibilities, expectations may not have been clearly articulated or timelines not specified. Maintain positive relationships by first asking and then listening to why something happened before blaming or asking for corrective action.

The importance of relationships will be brought to light during emergencies or difficult times. This is when you will need others or others will need you. If you don't have current relationships that you can rely on during bad times, you may want to rethink how you interact with others and what is missing. Modify your behavior and your commitment for building relationships to carry you through good times and bad.

Investing Time

Recognize that relationships take time. It takes time for others to get to know you and develop the trust and respect to commit to your ideas and follow you. It will also take time for you to grow relationships and get to know others to successfully lead them. However, with the multitude of priorities being placed on everyone, there is often a push to rush efforts and not allow sufficient time. It is vital to follow these steps:

1. Slow down;
2. Reflect; and
3. Focus on relationships.

Slowing down is critical so you don't miss important moments in relationship building. Until relationships and trust develop, those who don't know you well may perceive you differently than those who do. They won't understand your leadership style, sense of humor, priorities, or values, and you won't know theirs. Misunderstandings can easily develop, causing hurt feelings or defensive behavior that could cause permanent damage in the relationship. You will need to proceed with caution or provide more explanations until relationships have formed. The slower approach will provide an opportunity to assess what may be going on and to build stronger, trusting relationships.

When thinking about developing or enhancing your relationships, think about how you can build rapport. Find out what others are interested in, what excites them, and then help them nurture those interests. Take the time to understand what is going on with those around you. There are often stressors in their personal lives that can impact their behavior. If you are not aware of the circumstances, you may misunderstand their behavior and appear to be insensitive. Being sensitive and considering how others feel is a mark of empathic leadership.

When starting a new role or learning a new task, meet the people involved first. More than likely, they are experienced individuals who have attempted to make changes or who may not see the benefit to change. You will need to gain their trust in order to gain their commitment to your ideas. Spend time with them to understand their strengths, priorities, values, skills, and needs. Focus on building the relationships and trust. Identify any potential issues that need to be addressed. Never engage individuals in a manner that will cause them to be defensive. Be sensitive to their views and ideas, and offer recognition and an appreciation for what they have been doing.

Networking

Relationships will be developed by taking the initiative to meet people in other roles. This networking provides an exceptional opportunity to identify the various connections others may have with your role and responsibilities. When meeting with others, show a genuine interest in learning about their strategies and the opportunities they are working on. Share your background so that others know how you may be able to assist. Take time to build a network, without using it as a self-serving strategy.

Networking is an extremely vital competency to have. You can use your network in political ways, to help you get what you want. However, thinking of it in a different context will provide new insights. Build your network also with those whom you have helped as a strategy to optimize your contributions. Develop your network this way and you will have an extraordinary "team" on your side. Don't be concerned about what others can do for you, as this opportunity will come in time. This approach is part of being a servant leader and of being a *mensch* (Yiddish word, which frequently means "a responsible and good person").

After accepting a new job or assignment, expand your network by identifying individuals who may have a direct or indirect lens on the topic. Meet with individuals who have been at the organization an extended period of time and identify what roles and responsibilities they have as well as the projects and challenges they are working on. Identify potential linkages with projects. Allow others the opportunity to meet you. You may also find commonalities regarding where they previously worked or lived, or similar hobbies and interests. Friendships can be formed as well. Meeting people facilitates the "human" connection and adds more meaning to work.

The most likely way to find a new position or job is from your network. Have an extensive list of contacts in the event that you lose your job. Regularly take time to get involved in your industry, community, church, or synagogue, as well as hobbies. Help others with their careers. The broader your network is, the greater the chance that there will be an opportunity for you.

I used my network when, at a midpoint in my career, I found myself "in transition," looking for employment. Because I had been active in my professional association, the Medical Group Management Association (MGMA), I had many opportunities to engage individuals with whom I had interacted over the past 25+ years of my career. I connected with a colleague whom I had met and interacted with at MGMA annual meetings. When an opportunity presented at his organization, I had someone who could speak on my behalf and I was offered the job of my dreams as an administrator at Mayo Clinic where I still work.

Exhibit 2.1 offers more advice for developing relationships.

Professionalism

Professionalism can be defined as "Professional status, methods, character, or standards; conforming to the standards of a profession" (*American Heritage Dictionary* 2009). Therefore, it doesn't require being a professional but to behave according to the character and standards expected of professionals and the industry.

Professionalism can be characterized in many ways. One of my mentors told me that he rarely finds individuals who have all of

EXHIBIT 2.1 ■ Advice for Developing Relationships

Advice	Opportunity for Change
Don't be self-serving, talk just about yourself, ignore others, or become agitated, angry, or frustrated.	Serve others, and listen, be helpful, ask questions, remain calm, and be patient.
Don't ignore others' response to you. They may be signaling their doubts, distrust, or dislikes that will impact their respect for you and willingness to follow.	Think about how others will perceive you. Learn to "read your audience."
Don't use intimidation to try to influence others.	Develop trust and respect so others follow you by choice.
Don't be overly serious. No one wants to be around someone who is constantly stern or grim or doesn't have a sense of humor.	Pay attention to the level of "seriousness" you display. It is important to maintain a lightness and humor or even show playfulness at times.
Don't be sensitive or defensive in the face of criticism or negative feedback. Becoming defensive may make you the center of the issue and draw attention away from a potential resolution. Defensiveness may also negatively impact your relationship with others and result in less people approaching you with advice.	Accept feedback and learn from it. Develop a thick skin using confidence and reflection to handle and learn from criticism. Know that leaders can't be liked by everyone all the time because they must make tough decisions.
Don't be overly critical or provide inappropriate feedback. Never be harsh in providing advice, feedback, or recommendations to others.	Always offer feedback with the goal of helping the other individual, with a genuine interest in helping them as an end, not as a means to an end. Recognize when it's appropriate to offer constructive advice.
Do not be judgmental with individuals. Judgments are based on values, and values are personal. Being judgmental is likely to result in a defensive response by others to protect what is important to them.	Understand others' values and where they are coming from.
Don't overreact when others are being negative, incompetent, misinformed, or mean spirited. Don't respond to these negative reactions.	Minimize your time with others who are continuously toxic with negative thoughts. Remain positive or neutral.
Don't place talented individuals on a pedestal.	All individuals have flaws and will make mistakes, even your mentors and "heroes."

the following characteristics: (1) capable, (2) hard working, and (3) sensitive to others. These may be the triad of ingredients that could define a professional. Professionals have confidence, flexibility, resilience, and they demonstrate leadership skills. Other characteristics of professionals include:

- Having a tolerance for frustration;
- The ability to identify and focus on priorities;
- Maintaining a healthy work–life balance for continuous renewal; and
- The ability to navigate challenges and obstacles.

Professionals rarely have to find something to do because they are usually on a continuous quest for higher degrees of excellence. They recognize the importance of learning from others to inspire new connections, complement existing knowledge, and foster the development of new approaches to leadership. Accordingly, they have reading lists of books and other materials to learn from during quiet times or when there is a need to take a break.

A professional is able to reflect on experiences and knowledge obtained over the years and apply previous discoveries to new situations. The combination of reflection and learning enables professionals to arrive at conclusions and decisions when faced with new questions. The execution and results will be judged by others, but leaders will continue to reflect on their own decisions and the results for applying to future situations.

Professionalism will be interpreted based on your conversation, appearance, actions, and presentation of information. You need to constantly be aware of the way that you are presenting yourself in front of others.

Strategies for Maintaining Professionalism

The concept of professionalism is easy to understand but harder to actually conform to its standards. Displaying a high level of professionalism will be particularly noticeable when presented with enormous challenges, changing paradigms, constant complaining, or huge stressors. It is during these times that leaders will be tested. This is also when others will recognize your talents, not when you're addressing the routine issues. Be ready for the challenge.

Professionals have an arsenal of competencies, relationships, resources, and preparation available to handle all situations in a calm, effective manner. Stress and high-pressure situations don't result in emotional reactions. Achieving excellence with a calm, nonstressful manner will be appreciated, recognized, and rewarded. Strive to always act professionally and aspire to very high expectations.

Professionalism is critical for relationship and reputation building. Maintain the highly professional approach at all times. Every comment, word, reaction, and behavior is a display of your leadership attributes. Language, body language, mannerisms, and physical presence all convey messages. Reflect on the image you portray: the combination of what you do and say, how you present yourself, and what you accomplish. Be mindful of the integration of all these aspects in developing your level of professionalism.

When considering the type of leader you aspire to be, consider the virtues of faith, hope, charity, courage, justice, prudence, and temperance. Professionals are oftentimes characterized as those with the following positive attributes or competencies: visionary, stress tolerant, skilled communicator, organized, caring, and optimistic. Professionals demonstrate an inquiring and listening mind; using the knowledge they have acquired is what sets them apart. Consider each of these and other traits of professionalism as capabilities that can be learned, developed, and utilized.

One of the tabs in my life planner includes a list of specific behaviors that display professionalism. During moments of reflection or during meetings with others, I review the specific behaviors as teaching moments for myself and others.

A professional is going to exhibit a calm, patient, mindful, and considerate pacing rather than a frantic, panicked approach to issues. Wisdom is much more likely to be obtained in the former than the latter. You will conserve your energy as well. Continue to display a high level of professionalism, not frustration, anger, or other negative emotions.

Take the long view of excellence. A one-time success will not justify poor performance elsewhere, and a one-time lapse in judgment or performance should not spiral into a negative view of your capability. Consider the overall results being achieved with an eye toward improvement and a willingness to adjust strategies. Continuously ask the question, "How can the bar for excellence be raised?" Completing the task and achieving the goal will be appreciated and celebrated. However, there should be a continuous focus on what could have been done better and how the performance could be carried out.

Professionals are accountable for their actions and those of others under them. A "no blaming or shaming" approach needs to be dominant when looking at situations that could have been handled better. At times this may be the result of poor performance or decisions on your part. Acknowledge what happened, accept responsibility, learn from it, and share what you have learned. Holding others accountable is also part of the role of a professional, but helping them turn it into a learning opportunity will encourage their growth and can benefit the organization.

There might be circumstances when you may become involved in a dispute and others are displaying impolite, disrespectful, obnoxious, or aggressive behavior. It is particularly important to maintain a professional response and not be "dragged" into unprofessional arguments. Exhibit 2.2 lists recommendations for maintaining professionalism.

Listening

Listening may be the least recognized of the necessary competencies for leaders. Leaders are expected to talk, to direct meetings, and to present their ideas. The importance of listening is not recognized enough. Listening is a critical skill in leadership for two reasons:

1. It is through listening that leaders learn from others; and

2. Relationships are built and maintained by listening to others.

EXHIBIT 2.2 ■ Advice for Maintaining Professionalism

Advice	Opportunity for Change
Don't tell others what to do, preach, draw attention to yourself, be philosophical, expect results too quickly, or have unrealistic goals for yourself or others.	Do ask questions, provide advice when asked, listen more, lower your profile, provide concrete ideas when asked, be more patient, and think strategically.
Don't show excessive nervousness or let this interfere with your performance. Excessive nervousness is not likely to instill a sense of professionalism or confidence.	Display confidence and control or accept your nervousness. It is understandable to be nervous, especially in new situations.
Don't expect to know all the answers, and do not become frustrated if presented with a challenging issue	Reflect on past decisions, be familiar with the industry's body of knowledge, and leverage your network to know how to arrive at an answer.
Don't complain.	If you see something to complain about, look for solutions instead.
Don't become defensive when faced with unfair or inaccurate criticism.	Be unwavering in your level of professionalism. Let these situations be your growth opportunities. Rather than succumb, ruminate, or obsess, instead choose the higher road of listening, responding appropriately, and reflecting on why the negative reaction developed.
Don't allow extreme passion that can lead to unrealistic or unprofessional outbursts of excessive emotion.	Although passion and enthusiasm are virtues, passion also has bounds of acceptability. Be passionate to generate enthusiasm in you and others, but display it in appropriate levels.
Never gossip or make a negative comment about anyone. The comments could be quoted by others and be used against you.	Express opinions with others as though you were on an "open microphone." Consider how you word your messages to communicate in a less negative and more constructive manner. Model the highest level of leadership: respect for others. Maintain your professionalism.

There is a tendency to think that leaders' contributions are a result of their talking, expressing their opinions or decisions. Although it is important to express opinions and thoughts, listening is the portal to learning. You cannot learn from others' experiences, knowledge, and opinions if you aren't listening.

Learn to recognize when sharing your views will be helpful and contribute to team goals and when it will be more important to listen to others. Think of it like playing basketball: shoot the ball if you've got control and a clear shot, otherwise pass the ball to a team member who has a better shot. Similarly, talk if you have something important to share, otherwise listen.

Listening is also important to build and maintain your relationships. Listening to others may be the ultimate sign of respect: caring about others. Listening requires an appropriation of your time, placing the needs of another as your only point of focus, even if for just a few moments. You show your respect and interest in other people by listening to what they have to say and what is going on in their life and by prioritizing their needs over yours.

Strategies for Effective Listening

Sample Journal Entry

June 1: It might be a good time to spend more time listening vs. giving my opinion. I have been a bit too agitated and poetic in my characterizations. I should be more humble and make suggestions with more calmness. I will lose credibility by over-dramatizing, even if I am right.

When faced with a challenge or a new question, the process for resolving the issue is to learn through reading and your network of relationships. However, you won't learn from what you read or from your network if you don't listen to these resources. When meeting with your mentors and colleagues and presenting your questions, concerns, and ideas, remember to really listen to their advice or opinions and not just for confirmation of what you want or expect to hear. Listen for ideas, lessons from past experiences, cautions, or opinions that you should consider and incorporate. Listen to and reflect on others' comments prior to discounting them or moving on.

Listening empathetically and mindfully will increase your ability to understand the feelings of others and the information they want to convey. Listen to learn, to understand, and to be helpful and supportive. Listen with your heart, not just your mind.

Listen, knowing that you need to "hear" the feelings, not just the words. Listen with an open mind, with a consideration that you may come to different conclusions based on what you hear. Listen with the goal of finding the appropriate response to their needs without over- or underreacting.

A life epiphany on the importance of listening occurred when I was attending a suicide prevention course. The minister who was presiding explained that the most important role that he played in supporting a woman whose family member had just committed suicide was to listen. Discussing this situation and some criticism I had recently been receiving about not listening to colleagues at work, the pastor shared that I could help others more by listening for *feelings* not just words.

Know that there are times in relationships when others just need you to listen; not react, just listen; not judge, just listen. At times, the cathartic effect of talking will be the only benefit for the talker, but it will be important.

It is important to maintain your presence while listening. Your mind can start to wander; to think about how to justify or defend your views or what tasks are waiting for you. When your mind wanders, listening is reduced, impacting your appreciation of another's views and concerns. You must maintain focus on the other person, what they are saying and demonstrating in body language, in order to truly understand what is being conveyed.

When others are angry or frustrated, taking the time to listen can be helpful, especially if they just have a need to blow off steam. Listen with empathy while maintaining composure to reduce the high emotion of the moment. Use active listening to determine if there are underlying reasons for their emotions. Understand the reason for their anger and whether or not they are seeking answers or just venting.

If others are seeking answers from stress created by organization-based causes, explain the situation and reasons. For reasons triggered by situations in their personal life, be compassionate and have a presence for their release of emotion. Know when it is appropriate to offer sympathetic comments and when to kindly suggest they seek psychological counseling or career coaching.

EXHIBIT 2.3 ■ Advice for Effective Listening

Advice	Opportunity for Change
Don't let your mind wander while listening to others.	Maintain your focus on the speaker.
Don't do the talking when you are supposed to be listening.	Listen to what others are saying and listen carefully to help them or learn from them. Don't be thinking about what you want to say to justify or defend your views when you should be listening.
Don't be judgmental or preachy.	Listening requires an approach that is nonjudgmental and without preaching. Your emphasis is on listening, not commenting.
Don't be prejudiced or let prejudices lead to a prejudging of something or someone.	Maximize learning by eliminating prejudice. Listen to the views, opinions, and rationale with an open mind.

Listening is not possible unless there is engagement. So, being approachable is critical to achieving the type of engagement that will result in helpful exchanges. Having positive relationships encourages interaction, which reinforces relationships. This cycle is repeated continuously, which leads to your credibility as a leader. Listening is a vital key in this process.

If you are a good listener, co-workers, friends, family, and individuals who are parts of your network may be more likely to reciprocate to learn about your feelings and thoughts. This is how high-performance teams are developed.

Take the time to listen to feedback from your team. Others will have different insights, information, or advice based on their experiences and viewpoints, even if you worked on the same project. Ask about and listen to what you might have done better. Exhibit 2.3 lists suggestions for effective listening skills.

Conflict

The modern workplace has many opportunities for conflict to develop with the interaction of many different systems, processes, people, and work units. However, conflict, if not managed, is harmful to relationships and organizations, and can be a tremendous source of anxiety, interfering with morale and productivity. It impacts communication because listening shuts down, and negative emotions, such as anxiety and anger, can take center stage. Conflicts can disrupt and interfere with relationships.

This is where professionalism and the attributes of effective leadership are tested. In order to resolve or avoid conflict, it is necessary to understand the potential sources of conflict. Conflict can develop for a variety of reasons including:

- Poor communication;
- Differences in goals or objectives;
- Differences in personalities, values, and/or desires;
- Personal or work issues creating stress; or
- Trying to blame others when things go wrong.

Oftentimes, the situation is complicated by a confluence of factors creating a "chaos" of competing ideas, thoughts, feelings, and stressors. The underlying causes need to be isolated to identify the best means to diffuse the conflict.

Many want to avoid conflict rather than face it. Conflict is unsettling and many individuals will avoid or suppress a conflict with gestures, words, or other means to cover up the issue. Unfortunately, if these avoidance measures just mask the underlying issues, the potential for conflict may always remain. This suppression of emotions could lead to an explosion of feelings at a later time. Leaders need to constantly assess themselves and others to determine whether there are underlying issues that are suppressed but have the potential to create conflict in the future. Unless they are addressed, even minor or easily resolved disagreements can cascade into conflicts that cause permanent damage to relationships and the effectiveness of teams.

Strategies for Resolving Conflict

Frequently, it is the reaction to the disagreement or conflict that causes permanent damage and not the original cause of the conflict itself. Don't perpetuate the problem with inappropriate behavior. Real differences in values, goals, or objectives must be addressed, not ignored or swept aside. Conflict between others must be recognized and overcome, even if you must allow time for anger and frustration to cool prior to tackling the source of the disagreement.

Before reacting emotionally when conflict is developing, reflect by learning, trying to understand the situation and what caused it, and then identify an appropriate response or solution. Benefit from the wisdom that resulted from past conflicts: what caused them, how did you react, and how should you have reacted?

As previously mentioned, poor communication is a frequent cause of conflict. Consider where communication may have been derailed in the events leading up to the conflict. This is where slowing down and engaging in dialogue may be very helpful. Give the benefit of the doubt to the other person; remember: "innocent until proven guilty." Reach out to assess if you are part of the issue with poor communication. Ask yourself: "Did I communicate this clearly? Were my instructions unclear or conflicting?" Remember to ask for information or instructions to be repeated to ensure they are correctly received to limit the chance of conflict.

Poor communication can also result in one of your comments being received in an unintended manner. Did it cause hurt or defensiveness? There is a delicate balance between honesty and prudence. Although it might be ideal to be able to say what is on your mind, anytime, with anyone, this is not reality. Imagine being a politician when everything you say is recorded and interpreted. Always be mindful of how the other person will perceive what you say and be ready to acknowledge if something was interpreted in an unintended manner.

Another reason for conflict is the presence of different goals or desires in others. Disagreement can be healthy to create awareness that there are competing goals, perspectives, or values. Once you know that there is a disparity, don't let it create conflict. Instead, start a dialogue to learn others' perspectives on the issue. Discuss differences in goals, objectives, or values in order to determine where there is commonality and agreement and how to manage conflict.

The approach of "seek first to understand," as discussed by Stephen Covey (1989) in *The 7 Habits of Highly Effective People*, is

exceptionally powerful in conflict resolution. Once you understand, it will be easier to find agreement or new approaches that
can resolve the conflicting viewpoints.

Recognize that ideas you are suggesting may attack the very core
of the identity of others and their sense of worth. Not considering these potential obstacles is naïve and will result in ineffective
and inefficient change management. You should take a mindful
approach to these issues to identify and strategize about how
to overcome them. Develop a game plan in a calm, professional
manner to show that you respect others and their concerns but
assert the reasons for the change. They still may not see the
benefit or share your enthusiasm for a new idea or reason for
change, but more will be accomplished with a positive, question-
ing, compassionate attitude.

That is not to say that everyone is going to be in agreement all
the time, but you can use dialogue to manage the disagreement,
to show mutual respect, or to agree to disagree. Accept that
disagreement is not a bad thing, even with a superior. Leaders
soliciting feedback and the opinions of others should understand that dissenting opinions are needed for the benefit of the
organization and effective teamwork. Different opinions should
be expressed in a respectful manner with supporting evidence.
The opinions of others should be noted, appreciated, considered,
and evaluated. It is never appropriate to dismiss someone else's
thoughts without consideration, which is disrespectful.

The best offense for conflict management is to already have
outstanding relationships. This becomes particularly helpful in
stressful situations. When relationships are not healthy, there is
much more likelihood that circuitous communication or suppression of feelings are going to occur. Excellent relationships
will minimize the conflicts if there is a foundation of trust and
faith in each other. Little "offenses" will be accepted or ignored,
and major concerns are more likely to be aired and discussed.

There will be circumstances that are tense but haven't developed
into a conflict. Your reaction to the situation may determine if
the potential conflict escalates or not. At times, it may be better
to wait out an issue because it is a temporary phenomenon and
will resolve itself or you will realize that you are making more
of an issue than it deserves. While this is not to justify conflict

avoidance, sometimes there is benefit to allowing a natural cooling-off period. During the cooling-off phase, you can collect your thoughts, determine the underlying influences, and decide whether or not there is a reason to address the issue or if it will dissipate as a matter of course.

I was faced with a conflict years ago when I requested an additional manager in the specialty I was leading who would focus on specific aspects of developing the practice. I was denied the request multiple times because clinic leadership wanted to minimize the number of managers, and the role did not exist anywhere in the organization. Rather than escalate the conflict, I used a calm, methodical approach explaining the specific tasks of the position supported by financial evidence that the request would be an investment rather than a cost. I aligned the benefits to specific strategic objectives and strategies developed by top leadership. With patience rather than conflict and a year of "negotiating," the new manager position was approved and this role was extremely successful. Persuasion and patience were critical to achieve approval.

Exhibit 2.4 offers advice for resolving conflict.

Assertiveness

Observations

Assertiveness is a critical leadership skill. When placed in positions of leadership, it is expected that you will assert your opinion. Not sharing your knowledge and advocating for your opinions is unprofessional and shows a lack of leadership. Others are counting on you or you would not have been selected as a leader.

What makes it challenging is finding the balance between assertiveness and stronger, more negative behaviors. Others may perceive the assertiveness of a results-oriented, driven personality as intimidating or aggressive. However, trying to avoid being seen as aggressive or pushy could lead to the opposite: being viewed as passive or subordinate. It is important to find the balance between aggressiveness and passivity.

EXHIBIT 2.4 ■ Advice for Resolving Conflict

Advice	Opportunity for Change
Don't come to conclusions prematurely.	Remain open-minded. Seek the causes of the conflict. Give the benefit of the doubt to the other individual.
Don't let issues simmer until they explode into conflict.	Know when an issue needs to be addressed before it leads to excessive conflict. Approach these situations in a calm, controlled manner. Also recognize when issues will dissipate on their own and then let them fade.
Don't exhibit strong, negative emotions. This response may escalate the conflict and inhibit the results you seek. Don't personalize the conflict.	Maintain a composure and level of professionalism; display your leadership traits. This is a choice; control your thoughts and emotional reaction.
Don't become defensive; it creates barriers to resolving the issue and reduces the opportunity to learn.	Remain open to receiving and evaluating different ideas and consider them as possible solutions.
Don't become judgmental or argumentative.	Try first to understand the others' viewpoints, values, and objectives. Ask questions to identify areas of agreement as well as disagreement.
Don't react impulsively or emotionally.	Remain calm, reflective, sensitive, and positive.
Don't try to control the decisions made by others.	Control your reaction to others and their decisions. Be disciplined about the expenditure of effort and energy considering your goals.

Strategies for Appropriate Use of Assertiveness

When you approach others, reflect on using the right approach at the right time. Develop an assertiveness that is firm, confident, competent, and sensitive. Consider how your approach may be received so you come across as assertive, not aggressive or abrasive. Being abrasive will not be helpful. Being aggressive may be required, but rarely. A sensitive, confident assertiveness will likely be the most effective approach.

Being assertive does not mean pushing your views on others, nor does it mean being timid or caving in when resistance is encountered or an alternative idea is suggested. A balance must be found between asserting your opinion and remaining open to others' ideas or opinions. Being receptive to the ideas of others is an important leadership trait; at times the best way to display leadership is to follow rather than asserting your opinion.

There can be a risk to being assertive and speaking out in front of superiors, but there is also a risk not to. All leaders must have the ability to speak up or else suffer mediocrity. There are also case studies where problems have developed because individuals did not speak up and assert themselves. Crew resource management was developed in the airline industry as a result of catastrophes that occurred when flight crews did not question the captain in particular situations. In healthcare, staff members frequently did not challenge physicians until it was realized that speaking up can save lives. Team members need to be counted on to question or challenge leaders when a mistake is about to occur.

Maintaining assertiveness can be challenging when interacting with individuals who themselves are abrasive, aggressive, or intimidating. Their behavior may drive you to respond in a similar manner, escalating the emotion, or to back off and become passive. Backing off may divert the conflict but could also lead to more intimidation. Standing your ground may be the only way to avoid being taken advantage of, but the appropriate response will depend on the situation. Ask yourself: Is my stance worth fighting for? What is the position of the other individual? Standing up for your opinion will require well-presented supporting materials and, perhaps, a higher authority or support from elsewhere. There is no sense in being assertive if you can't defend your reasoning. Exhibit 2.5 offers recommendations for appropriate use of assertiveness.

Diversity and Inclusiveness

Diversification is one of the critical strategies in investment management. Since the future is unknown, investors manage diverse portfolios to try and counter the ups and downs of different types of investments (stocks, bonds, real estate, etc.). The intent is to reduce risk and increase the return on investment over the long term.

The same is true of the advantages of diversity and inclusiveness in the workplace and in your career. Research has demonstrated

EXHIBIT 2.5 ■ Advice for Appropriate Use of Assertiveness

Advice	Opportunity for Change
Don't maintain your opinion when it's inappropriate.	Recognize there are times when it makes more sense to accept the ideas of others.
Don't be afraid to be assertive when appropriate.	Lacking assertiveness may result in a perception that you do not have the skills to deal with difficult issues or people. Although it is important to be prudent, it is also critical to have courage when needed. Stand firm when it's appropriate.
Don't let your assertiveness grow into anger or lead to a fight.	Be prudent and temperate. Pick your battles wisely.
Don't display aggressiveness, insensitivity, or carelessness.	Take the time to reflect on how your assertiveness may appear to others.

that groups consistently outperform individuals. Groups can draw on the diverse knowledge, experience, and ideas of individual members to craft creative solutions and warn of potential hazards. Diversity is a source of innovation, one of the organizational drivers for excellence. However, this group concept can only be accomplished if others believe they are really being included in the discussions.

Diversity and inclusiveness in a team is like a balanced portfolio to increase the flexibility and response of the group with each member able to contribute at different times for different reasons. Much like music has evolved over time with the fusing of different types of music and instruments from different cultures, the same result occurs when bringing different ideas and individuals together, combining the unique contributions of team members.

Diversity of opinion is based on more than one's experience and knowledge. Think of a hologram in the center of a large room full of people. Does everyone have the same view of the hologram? No, because they are all looking at it from different angles. Metaphorically, we "look" at things differently because of our different "angles," influenced by our current view, history, fears, hopes, knowledge, aptitude, attitude, and our ability to visualize and imagine.

Diversity in your career, life, and learning experiences can have similar benefits. Accepting new positions will expose you to different leaders and co-workers plus various aspects of the industry or even of other industries. The exposure will also encourage you to develop a variety of skill sets and knowledge as you tackle new challenges. Having a greater repertoire of competencies and experiences will enhance your ability to adjust to changing circumstances.

Strategies for Diversity and Inclusiveness

Diversity, inclusiveness, creativity, and innovation are all vital aspects of leadership. New ideas are needed to achieve organizational excellence. This requires openness to the ideas of others and receptivity to potentially foreign concepts or suggestions. Ideas from others will be enhanced if they consider themselves included as vital members of the team. Diverse relationships and activities will influence a different type of thinking and learning that may result in creative and innovative solutions. Experiment by working with and learning from others and taking on new tasks or new roles.

The concept of diversity can generate many images such as age, race, and gender inclusion. Diversity and inclusiveness is also about knowledge, culture, learned behavior, experiences, and other factors making each individual unique. Having a diverse team ensures that a variety of skill sets are available and each skill set integrates with others, potentially creating a synergistic effect.

You need to encourage expression of different views to reap the benefits of diversity. The key to succeeding with diversity is being open and listening. As team members express their unique or even peculiar ideas, you must remain open-minded to their possibilities. If you close your mind to ideas other than those within the realm of your thinking or experiences, you defeat the benefits of diversity. Especially during initial strategy or planning sessions, encourage a free flow of ideas, no matter how far out they may seem there will be time to narrow the options later.

Diversity is beneficial in your career path and network as well. Malcolm Gladwell, in his book *Outliers: The Story of Success* (2008), proposes a concept of 10,000 hours required to become an expert in anything. Experts are critical to organizational development. However, there is a delicate balance that has to be struck between focusing energy to achieve the expert stage in any one thing vs. being open to gaining different experiences and gathering different views to maintain perspective and broaden your knowledge base. Accepting a variety of job opportunities will expose you to different aspects of the organization, the industry, and even of other industries. Even within one position there are benefits of seeking out new assignments, new responsibilities. Each new assignment will offer new challenges and the opportunity to develop new skill sets or to meet new colleagues.

Always seek new opportunities to increase the diversity within your network. New positions or community activities will increase the number of individuals with whom you can develop relationships. Meeting leaders in other industries or fields will expose you to entirely new ideas and advice. It is important to surround yourself with others who will not only help you learn from their experiences but also provide an honest opinion or warning when needed.

Look for learning opportunities to support a diversity of new knowledge and understanding. Broaden your reading and other learning sources. Use your leadership journal to record insights and inspirations that hit during these opportunities. Exhibit 2.6 provides a list of advice for diversity and inclusiveness.

Perspective

Problems are solved and progress is enhanced by having perspective: a realistic assessment of what is going on, considering all of the systems, processes, and environmental factors, and keeping an eye on the vision and goals. Perspective is the essence of systems thinking – the integration of it all.

A loss of perspective can easily occur after you have been doing something for a long time or if you are mired in details. Losing perspective is dangerous when larger issues or concerns are not identified or the task becomes more important than the goals and vision. Loss of perspective can also interfere with the ability

EXHIBIT 2.6 ■ Advice for Diversity and Inclusiveness

Advice	Opportunity for Change
Don't discount any opportunity in your career to expand your network or career experiences.	Diversify your learning opportunities by remaining open to new options.
Don't tolerate prejudices in yourself or others.	There is no room for prejudices for any reason in this increasingly diverse world. Speak up when others show intolerance.
Don't limit your team and network to those who share your ideas, a collection of "yes people."	Seek out a diversity of perspectives, experiences, and opinions, and really listen to what others say.
Don't ignore others because their personalities, mannerisms, or other factors irritate you.	Remain open to the opportunities to learn from these individuals. Be mindful of whether you are really including others.

to see shifting environmental (internal and external) conditions that no longer support previous approaches or decisions.

Maintaining perspective will also help carry one through the bad times with the ultimate goals in mind. Oftentimes, it is the appearance of stress-related health issues that highlight when perspective is lost. Times like these are opportunities to use reflection to regain perspective.

Strategies for Maintaining Perspective

Use humor, reflection, learning, and relationships to help you keep a sense of perspective. Remember that very few things are worth causing you to lose sleep or your health. Maintaining perspective and humor will enhance your professional performance and improve your attitude. Perspective will come over time with learning, successes, and mistakes.

Relationships with others should help in maintaining perspective. Your network can provide opinions and reminders that will help. Their advice, questions, and sense of humor can balance the tunnel vision or loss of perspective that you might develop. Reviewing the plan and tasks with others can also reaffirm the long-term goals and provide an awareness of progress that has been made.

Working in the healthcare field is very stressful and can lead to a tendency to be too serious in your work. A balance needs to be achieved to find the humor, playfulness, and joy to maintain perspective and the energy for sustained leadership effort. Use jokes, cartoons, artwork, celebrations, or whatever matches your leadership style and the organizational culture in order to bring lightness and humor to the workplace and your office.

Other strategies to maintain perspective include:

- Reflecting on past experiences;
- Focusing on the vision, strategies, and goals;
- Learning from reading leadership materials or about the industry;
- Reviewing plans and how much progress has been made; and
- Balancing work vs. play (or at least nonwork).

Maintaining the big picture view will keep you focused on the vision and the priorities. It can be easy to lose the focus, get buried in details, and make poor decisions. It is important to ensure that progress is made toward achieving goals and that individual tasks will support the long-term vision or mission. Sustaining an appropriate perspective will help you address the immediate crisis and guide you to identify alternate strategies.

Learn to accept that mistakes, roadblocks, and less-than-desirable results will occur. Babe Ruth was a home-run king, but he also was a strike-out king. While it is natural to consider some instances as failures or mistakes, you can convert everything into a lesson by maintaining perspective. Lessons don't stop when you leave school; life is the classroom.

Maintaining perspective will also help you in times of frustration, anger, disappointment, and conflict. Negative emotions are not needed. Keep a professional focus on achieving the desired results to avoid these types of reactions. Remind yourself that this is part of the leadership process.

When faced with frustration, disappointment, and crises, it is often helpful to step back and to assess what is going well. Life is a roller coaster of ups and downs. When you are facing a major challenge or crisis, don't forget about the other aspects of life that may be going very well and remember your true values. Remember how you overcame other challenges and crises. It is very easy to focus too much on what is not working. Keep perspective on all aspects and maintain a foundation of optimism.

The most significant experience of perspective for me personally was when I was 16 and experienced the death of my father. While others my age were thinking about going to the prom, I was dealing with a very somber event in my life. I experienced profound sadness at the time, but I have benefitted since then because the experience taught me to integrate perspective into all aspects of my life. Losses in life or at work can be a time for gaining or maintaining a perspective of what is truly important.

Perspective can be enhanced by obtaining information from a variety of reliable and trusted sources. Like sailors using different navigational devices (map, stars, and compass) to ensure that they are on course in the open seas, refer to your network, team members, literature, and leadership journal for advice, inspiration, and a sense of balance. This is particularly important with new assignments and emotionally challenging situations.

Gaining or maintaining perspective is a process of using systems thinking. Consider the short- and long-term impact of decisions. Think through the cause-and-effect relationships that exist. Consider how processes are working together as gears in a machine and how results are being generated. On the people side, consider the needs and desires of your colleagues in order to optimize engagement and commitment. Integrate your understanding of environmental variables that can impact decisions and results. Pull back from the details and put together the complete picture.

Part of being a leader is helping others maintain perspective. This includes helping employees and team members identify the organizational priorities and goals, even as they get caught up in individual tasks and details. It includes educating others as to why ideas they are advocating for are not being adopted or prioritized. Exhibit 2.7 offers advice for maintaining perspective.

EXHIBIT 2.7 ■ Advice for Maintaining Perspective

Advice	Opportunity for Change
Don't overreact. Overreaction can create a cascade of negative effects and emotions, including blinding you to potential solutions and damaging relationships.	Maintain control and perspective to respond with the appropriate reaction and the ability to logically identify the next steps to resolve issues.
Don't get hung up on smaller issues.	Remember the big picture and long-term goals. Take a reflective pause to reorient and regain the perspective. Not "sweating" the small stuff, as discussed in *Don't Sweat the Small Stuff at Work* by Richard Carlson (1998), is an example of maintaining perspective.
Don't forget your network.	Your relationships with mentors, family, and colleagues will help you maintain your orientation and identify priorities.
Don't forget the priorities in your life.	Regardless of what happens with your job, you still have other priorities, including your health and relationships with family and friends.

Conclusion

Developing and maintaining strong relationships and having great interpersonal skills will help you in achieving excellence as a leader. There is a lot to think about, learn, and practice related to developing and maintaining good relationships. It is helpful to occasionally pause and evaluate your interpersonal skills to assess how you are being perceived. The questions in Exhibit 2.8 may be useful to reflect on your behavior when it comes to working with others.

EXHIBIT 2.8 ■ Questions for Reflection: Developing Relationships

Relationships:	What strategies do you use to enhance your relationships? What mistakes have you made that have damaged relationships?
Professionalism:	What are the characteristics of professionalism that you admire most in others? How are you developing your professionalism?
Listening:	While listening, what strategies do you use to focus your attention on others? How do you maintain an open mind when listening to others?
Conflict:	How do you address personality conflicts? How do you address competing values?
Assertiveness:	How do you identify when it is appropriate to be assertive vs. letting others' ideas take priority? As a rule are you passive, passive-aggressive, aggressive, or assertive... honestly?
Diversity and Inclusiveness:	What strategies do you use to proactively search for ideas that are different from yours? How do you ensure that you are exposed to a diversity of opinions, ideas, and personal experiences?
Perspective:	When stressed by competing requests, how do you maintain a perspective on what is important? When others are being assertive advocating for their ideas, how do you help them maintain perspective on why other initiatives will take precedence?

Action items: What two or three specific actions will you commit to as a result of reading this chapter on Leading Others by Developing Relationships?

1. _____

2. _____

3. _____

Leading Organizations by Achieving Excellence

Integrated Leadership Model

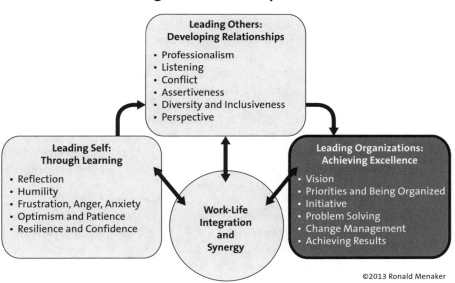

©2013 Ronald Menaker

Leading organizations is challenging in every industry. The extreme challenges facing healthcare leaders are exacerbated by many factors, including increasing costs and regulations, an aging population with chronic conditions, financing mechanisms that do not incentivize healthy living, waste in the healthcare industry, growing numbers of uninsured, a shortage of providers, rapidly changing technology, and so forth. National and state budget deficits and these industry realities are threatening the viability of many healthcare organizations.

Dealing with this multitude of challenges puts heavy demand on healthcare leaders. The pressure to succeed and meet the expectations of physicians and other stakeholders requires a high level of leadership excellence in all industry leaders. Achieving success for themselves and their organizations will require leaders to maximize their potential and rise to meet the challenge.

Excellence

Excellence is not going to appear one morning with a sign saying, "Done, you are excellent." Neither are you or the organization born "excellent." It is achieved by constant dedication to learning and improvement, disciplined thought and execution, and strategic assessment of the future. It is not something that is achieved once, like winning a race, and then you can relax. Excellence requires constant diligence and effort to maintain and to adapt to changing environments.

Excellence is not achieved overnight; it is the result of "putting it all together." It requires learning, reflection, experience, and all the characteristics previously described. It means leading yourself and building your network and relationships with others to achieve organizational excellence.

Excellence is not one-dimensional. It is about performing very difficult tasks at a very high level and being able to repeat the performance in good times and bad. Like the Olympic divers and gymnasts whose scores are based on the level of difficulty as well as the quality of the performance, leaders are evaluated based on the quality of their performance and the ability to lead during difficult times. Just as Olympic athletes are constantly developing new, increasingly difficult routines, leaders are also expected to take risks and not just take the safe, easy route.

Strategies for Achieving Excellence

Excellence is challenging because it requires a unique set of characteristics and vision in order to anticipate, understand, and address the challenges and changes of the healthcare industry and society. Excellence involves identifying, understanding, and cultivating strengths to achieve the long-term goals that you have set professionally, personally, and for the organization. It means constantly learning about yourself and the industry, assessing the environment to evaluate changes to prepare for the future. Without personal excellence, it will be difficult for the team and organization to achieve excellence.

Leaders should think of achieving excellence in three areas:

1. Personal excellence;
2. Leading your team to achieving excellence; and
3. Striving for organizational excellence.

Personal Excellence

Many characteristics are needed to achieve excellence; most can be learned and developed. Previously described characteristics and strategies include being optimistic, resilient, and patient, along with being able to listen, reflect, and manage conflict and negative emotions. Having good relationships and high levels of competence, energy, and endurance are also needed. Additional characteristics include:

- Having an inspirational vision;
- Being passionate about your job and industry;
- Having an ability to identify and set the correct priorities; and
- Knowing when the time is right to take action or make changes.

There exists a cycle that can lead to long-term excellence: learning → problem solving → results → confidence → learning. Learning improves your ability to solve problems. Each problem solved with good results builds confidence to attack the next challenge. Confidence reinforces the need for learning, and learning is the key to developing competence to stay on this cycle.

Excellence is a result of translating knowledge into action to obtain the desired results. Knowledge comes from the many years of study required for advanced professional positions along with lifelong learning about your field, business, and leadership. Think of life like school, with the constant threat of a "pop quiz" or final exams. Use the same strategy of learning, organizing, storing, and accessing knowledge so that you are constantly prepared and could take and pass the quiz or final exam at any time.

Coaches, mentors, and other resources are available to help in the process of learning to achieve personal excellence. Always listen to and heed the advice of others with more experience. Your network is always available to offer advice, answer questions, share insights, or to hear your ideas. You can also consider how the most experienced, enlightened, knowledgeable, and capable leaders you know would approach an issue. How would they approach the problem? What kinds of decisions would they make? Seek out your mentors and those in higher levels of leadership who have more or different experiences to provide a different perspective for making informed decisions.

Experience is needed to achieve excellence since it is not going to be reached the first time you do something. In fact, the first time may result in poor performance as a result of fear, inexperience, or insufficient knowledge. Consider each experience, learn from it, make changes, and monitor for improvements in order to raise your level of performance. Continue to reflect on past successes and errors, and then apply the knowledge to future performance. Many famous individuals have experienced huge failures and disappointments, but these experiences were typically instrumental in their future success. Also, with increased knowledge and experience, you will be able to adjust to emerging circumstances and modify decisions midstream.

Achieving excellence involves a complex integration of concepts: learning, focus, strategies, priority management, and a host of other factors. One critical aspect is in deciding what you will no longer do. This can be challenging, because traditions and habits may be difficult to change and these activities may be a source of identity and/or happiness. However, if you don't give up some of these ideas or activities, there may not be time or energy to create or adjust to the shifting paradigm. Giving up the old and transitioning to the new can be disorienting, but it is also required and should be embraced.

Excellence will be easier to achieve if you are passionate about your career, job, or endeavor. The flames of passion will generate the extra effort, the drive to go the extra mile, and keep you pushing the boundaries of knowledge, practice, and theory.

In his book *Good to Great: Why Some Companies Make the Leap... and Others Don't*, Jim Collins (2001) describes the need for passion to achieve the highest level of excellence. Those companies realized that success is more likely when you have identified that "space" they labeled as the hedgehog. To become a hedgehog, find out what is really needed, what you are really good at, what drives your passion, and what is economically rewarding. Allow time to get to know yourself and the efforts or opportunities that you enjoy the most. Pick your field of work very carefully to be authentic about what drives passion in your life, otherwise you are not likely to be committed enough to achieve the excellence. Then spend thousands of hours focusing your time, energy, and resources to develop yourself in this area. This will help you achieve the level of excellence you aspire to.

This conflicts with the idea that you also need to be knowledgeable about a variety of areas or to be a generalist. Both can be right; you just need to understand the trade-offs involved, the circumstances that you are in, and what is appropriate for your position. Having general knowledge and skills will also be beneficial at different stages in your career.

Last of all, remember that personal excellence requires rest and balancing/integrating work and life. Without periods of rest, damage will be done. Athletes training for competition and events can cause damage by overtraining. Music is enhanced by the "rests" or pauses between notes. Weight lifters build strength by alternating days of lifting, rest, and cross-training. Discipline is needed to rest and not work. Be mindful of downtime as much as work time.

Helping Others Achieve Excellence

As a leader, part of your responsibility is to help others achieve excellence. You cannot do it all yourself. Processes, change efforts, goals, decisions, and implementation all include strategies that require teamwork. Developing excellence in your colleagues benefits you and your organization and results from many factors including:

- Encouraging continuous learning;
- Coaching and mentoring;
- Setting high expectations;
- Delegating appropriate tasks to appropriate people;
- Holding individuals accountable; and
- Monitoring performance with clear metrics.

Recommend that employees seek out opportunities to increase their knowledge about the field and leadership through formal education programs, conferences, literature, and other means. Develop programs within the organization to offer mentoring and opportunities to learn more about the organization. Set high expectations that push individuals to gain more knowledge and develop more skills, but offer support to minimize the chance of failure. Delegate more responsibilities to improve the competencies in those around you so you can learn and benefit from their efforts.

Achieving excellence in others requires recognizing differences in individuals. You should consider the different aspects of thinking, feeling, judging, perceiving, and doing as described in personality assessments like the Myers–Briggs Type Indicator®. Utilize a contingency or situational approach to leadership by employing the most effective method for the individual with whom you are interacting given the situation. This will be much more effective than using just one approach. The master craftsman has considerably more tools in the "toolbox" than the weekend handyman.

Think of leading a team like playing in a rock band. To achieve excellence in a rock band you need to recognize the importance of timing, awareness of what other members of the band are doing, letting others take turns leading and following, agreeing on the rhythm and song selection, concentrating on the current song, and recognizing the importance of every musician. Many of these strategies are similar to those encountered with teamwork.

Striving for Organizational Excellence

Building an excellent organization takes time to achieve and requires a "one step at a time" process. Successes will be intermingled with the setbacks of failures and disappointments. This is why long-term, continuous improvement is needed. Like the planning and laying down of a foundation for a house, there is a lot of time and energy needed to lay the foundation for a successful organization and to ensure that all the parts are in place and ready. The parts include excellent leaders surrounded by high-performing teams.

Excellence is much more likely to be achieved with mindful prioritization and a relentless desire for improvement. This is not the subject matter for periodic planning retreats. Rather, this is a full-time orientation, a culture fixated on constant improvement. Jim Collins and Morten T. Collins wrote in the book *Great by Choice* (2011) about the successful companies who engage in the twenty-mile march, the consistent and calm quest for excellence. No glamour needed, just continued discipline and a focus on operational and strategic excellence.

Experienced leaders know that achieving excellence is also going to involve abandonment; in this case, abandonment of the old ways of doing things that are no longer optimizing the results. This does not mean that you abandon people, just disposing of ideas or products that are no longer contributing to the organization. Once excellence is achieved, processes and ideas must continually be reviewed to ensure that they are still relevant or if new ideas are needed in order to maintain or achieve a higher level of excellence.

However, the enemy of excellence is success and the complacency that tends to come with success. There is a natural tendency when a goal has been achieved to let up, to celebrate, to become complacent and/or focus on something else.

Complacency in an organization is especially dangerous in competitive environments, and nearly every environment is competitive. Although your organization may be achieving a level of excellence, competitors may be improving even more or coming out with the next hot product. Many businesses have relaxed after developing the latest "must have" product only to watch as competitors passed them by and made them obsolete. In a turbulent, disruptive environment, this can happen rapidly, leaving no time for correction. Keep the focus on a continuous quest for higher levels of performance and ensuring your product or service keeps up with customer needs. This can be especially difficult when faced with bureaucracies; there can be a tendency to become more focused on managing the bureaucracy instead of being innovative. Executives and others should constantly ask the questions, "What would raise the bar on performance?" and "What must we do next to enhance our success?" Exhibit 3.1 lists recommendations for achieving excellence.

Vision

Having a long-term vision is a powerful strategy for a leader. An inspiring vision will generate passion and drive to achieve the goal and a high level of excellence. Sharing an inspiring vision can have a powerful impact, like a magnet, in drawing the engagement of others. It provides a constant light, like a lighthouse, guiding you and your organization through the turbulence of today's environment. If others are inspired by and share your vision, they will commit their energy and passion to help you achieve common goals.

The challenge of creating a vision is that it requires an ability to see considerably down the road. You are being asked to prepare for a future without a clear map or being able to predict the ups, downs, and changes that always threaten to derail future plans. The process of developing the vision should open your eyes and mind to perceive future trends and factors that will impact achieving the vision.

Strategies for Developing Vision

Leaders should consider developing both a personal and an organizational vision. Personal visions identify the goals for your career and life. They are used to determine priorities for your time and energy and as a basis to evaluate choices that you will be faced with. Without a vision, you can fall into the trap of over-commitment because each request may have some benefit but may distract you from the major priorities and vision. You should evaluate each request as to whether it will advance you

EXHIBIT 3.1 ■ Advice for Achieving Excellence

Advice	Opportunity for Change
Don't believe that just working harder will help you achieve excellence.	Working smarter and smarter is the key. Keep asking if time and energy are being optimized, ask better questions, listen, and learn more.
Don't think you will achieve perfection.	Even excellence is not going to result in perfect performance all the time. Mistakes and errors in judgment will take place. This is where resilience and self-confidence are needed.
Don't avoid the chance of making mistakes by being overly cautious.	Although you can reduce the chance of making mistakes by avoiding risky decisions, you will not realize the benefits of trying something new or learning from the process. Excellence is developed by learning from mistakes as well as successes.
Don't settle for checking off the "to do" or task list.	With each completed task, ask the question of whether excellence has been achieved: Was the process completed in the best possible manner? It is much better to aim higher than to settle for average.
Don't spread yourself too thin.	Excellence involves choice between needs, hobbies, interests, family and friends, work and professional obligations. Make conscious choices on where to devote energy and to achieve excellence.
Don't get impatient with the effort to achieve excellence.	Patience is important because frustration often sets in with the slow pace of progress and change. Allow excellence to build and develop in yourself and your organization.
Do not confuse excellence with appreciation.	Many times excellent work will not be recognized. Individuals may not take the time to share appreciation or recognition. This should not be taken personally. Professionals achieve excellence without a need for recognition because of the internal reward for achieving excellence.
Don't let the challenges of stress, overwork, competing priorities, boredom, disappointment, or distractions deter you from achieving excellence.	Develop strategies to prevent negative reactions from occurring and know how to address them if and when they appear. Use your passion to focus energy and dedication, or consider other options if you have lost your passion.
Don't sit back and rest on your accolades.	Maintain constant diligence to sustain excellence, prepare for the future, and stay ahead of the competition.

toward the vision. Your vision will help you identify whether you should pursue additional education, accept a new job offer, develop additional competencies, or devote more time to your family or personal endeavors to make your vision come true.

The organizational vision sets the foundation for all future decisions with regard to organizational priorities. Priorities determine the goals and strategies and how resources will be committed to achieving them, including the distribution of resources such as labor, technology, marketing, and finance. Effectively, all decisions should be based on whether or not it will move the organization closer to the vision. Having a vision with strong implementation strategies, accountability, and metrics of success will improve the probability of achieving excellence.

Effective organizational visioning requires teamwork to draw out the experiences, diversity, and passion of others. Encourage people to see a positive, inspiring image of the future rather than being trapped by history. Stretch the comfort zone with a new and challenging but achievable goal. The team is more likely to succeed if it has a synergy to effectively exchange information and ideas in order to develop and achieve a sound, inspiring vision. The process should also include discussion and debate to decide on strategies to achieve the vision.

Visions and goals should be expressed in positive terms to be most inspiring. People want to be attracted to something, not reminded of actions they should not take. Focus on the do's, the positive imagery. Take time to ensure that the vision statement is clearly and accurately expressed. The clearer the vision, the easier it will be for others to commit to it and to identify relevant information to shape actions.

Evaluate visions periodically to ensure that they are still valid and relevant. Personal visions may need to be modified based on changing passions, opportunities, or circumstances. The organizational vision may need to be modified if the future or the environment is different than anticipated. Evaluate the reason for changing the vision to ensure that it is not based on the latest whim. Solid, valid reasoning should provide the foundation for making changes to the vision statement. Exhibit 3.2 offers more advice for developing vision.

EXHIBIT 3.2 ■ Advice for Developing Vision

Advice	Opportunity for Change
Don't forget to develop and explicitly share your vision.	Without vision, you and your organization may not have the drive and goals needed to excel. Instead, you may be distracted by whims and changing short-term goals.
Don't stray from the vision.	Focus on the vision. Keep your eyes on the target, adjusting along the way.
Don't remain locked onto a vision that is no longer valid.	Recognize when a vision needs to be changed or discarded. If the future the vision was based on is no longer true, the vision will not help you achieve excellence.
Don't assume that others will know the vision or quickly and easily understand it.	Over-communicate in sharing the vision by soliciting, engaging, and inspiring others along the way.

Priorities

Because there are always many things competing for time, attention, and/or money, it is necessary to define priorities, both personal and organizational. Establishing priorities focuses individual and organizational attention and resources to those issues that have been identified as critical for future success. It is conceptually easy but difficult to implement because of shifting priorities from leaders, "fires" that flare up demanding immediate attention, turnover of key staff members or executives, the appearance of new opportunities, and priorities in one's personal life.

Priorities should be based on values and vision; other items are either incidental or less important but they cannot *all* be priorities. Priorities should be a constant reminder, especially when faced with overwhelming obstacles or challenges, of the long-term vision and the plan to achieve it. Determine priorities by identifying the critical strategic and operational issues for the long term. Ask yourself, "Does the option or initiative align with the mission and does it move the organization closer to the vision?" This requires discipline.

Strategies for Setting Priorities

There can be an infinite amount of demands on your time and work that needs to be done. Accordingly, it is imperative to have a prioritization methodology for projects and workload. Work and demands will come from a variety of sources, but there is only one prioritizer...you. Only you will know about all of the inflows of requests and demands. It is up to you to determine the importance and schedule of each demand for your time and attention.

Making important decisions is often painful. You can be seduced by what may appear to be a great opportunity. This is when articulated priorities and values can be particularly helpful. Sticking to established priorities will focus your attention on those issues that have been identified as critical to future success. Weigh the opportunity against the stated mission, vision, and values...objectively and honestly. Is it a priority and will it carry you further down the path toward achieving the organization's vision and goals? By answering this question, you will increase the chances that you will make the right decision.

Besides setting priorities, other tools to help you accomplish what should be done include rescheduling of priorities, process or structural redesign, and delegation. These are all positive, adaptive changes and much more likely to result in improved and desired results than the other options such as becoming overwhelmed, quitting your job, or suffering consequences to your health, marriage, or other relationships.

When thinking about organizational priorities, think about the three Ps: people, process, and productivity...in this order. Always place people as the most important priority of the organization. Then focus on process, ensuring that the process contributes to the vision and priorities and that people are spending their time effectively and efficiently on the process. If you have been effective in considering people and process, productivity will almost always result. Also, you will not give the wrong message that "it is all about money" or that the goal is to make people work harder.

The presence of an effective strategic plan, outlining the long- and short-term goals, is necessary to provide guidance on priorities for decisions. Strategic planning should be conducted to identify strategies on the path to achieving the vision and excellence, and to minimize lower-priority projects.

When working with others, help them identify the priorities or limit the number of projects they are working on so they can focus their resources, energy, and efforts to achieve the desired results. Otherwise, diffused efforts on too many projects can result in compromised quality, delayed results, or confusion as to what are the actual priorities.

I'm called upon frequently to assist others in strategic planning. After affirming mission vision, and values, we conduct a SWOT assessment of the strengths, weaknesses, opportunities and threats. Suggestions are then offered for potential initiatives to move the organization closer to the vision. A critical part of this process is to then prioritize the degree of support and the importance of each of these potential initiatives. This voting process helps to limit the number of initiatives in order to focus energy and attention.

Remember that priorities can shift as opportunities are presented and life's journey unfolds. From time to time, this may require evaluating priorities, consciously lowering some so that others can be raised. This is true at work and home.

Priority and Time Management

Priority management is extremely important, especially in stressful environments. If the workload was less, there would be more opportunity for completing work on time and with a comfortable pace. However, it is more typical for the work demand to be extensive. Without enough time and too many demands, priorities need to be more carefully managed. The mechanism to prioritize your efforts is often called time management, but it is really priority management.

Time management is easier if you have a clear picture of what you are trying to achieve and are alert to factors impeding progress so you can do something about them. You can become more efficient by increasing your knowledge and competencies (to lessen your energy expenditure) and developing your relationships (to have others help you).

Learn to manage and prioritize the flow of requests that come from multiple stakeholders including physician partners, administrative leaders, and employees. Different individuals will have different priorities, based on their values/concerns/vision/fears. Be explicit and clear in determining the priorities of others and how they integrate with your existing priorities.

Other strategies for time management include reduce unnecessary work and distracters, delegate to others, and focus activities on results. Continuously ask the question, "Am I optimizing the way I spend my time?" Optimal time management (to achieve the desired results) requires a constant reevaluation of how time is being spent, eliminating waste that inevitably creeps into processes and daily activities. Taking out waste will raise performance to higher levels.

Time is rarely going to be available, so waiting for enough time for a task or project is not realistic. Rather, be proactive and identify what needs to be accomplished and prioritized. Assess the processes being used and the individuals on the team and their capabilities. Individuals and teams can be creative to complete tasks within the time given, especially if they have been involved in the process of visioning and establishing priorities.

As responsibilities expand, it is imperative to delegate more. Ask "Does this task need to be done by me?" Taking the time to develop others will result in more opportunities to delegate as your staff will have additional capabilities. By delegating more, you may be able to take on more responsibility and contribute in other ways. Delegation becomes even more important when you are assigned additional responsibilities, as this can provide an opportunity to develop others. Thus, the cycle is develop, delegate, and contribute, and you will evolve from being a "do-er" to a manager of results.

Make efficient use of time by knowing how your body, mind, and personality operate. Discover whether you are more creative in the morning or whether you are a "night person." Identify the optimal time to do different types of tasks most effectively. For example, a "morning person" may be much more productive working on creative or difficult problems first thing in the day, with routine meetings held in the afternoon when one is less energetic or creative. You may want to schedule specific time for certain types of activities (responding to e-mails, reflection or development time) that can either enhance your productivity and creativity or align with the strategic plan.

Time management will be more effective if you can select the appropriate solution and resources. To resolve an issue, there are times to use a sledge hammer, a mallet, or a thumb tack. Using a sledge hammer when you needed a thumb tack is an incredible waste of time and resources. Providing a simple solution (thumb tack) to an enormously complex issue is naïve and not helpful or effective. Simpler solutions are usually smoother and quicker to implement but may not last. Use a scoping process to make an appropriate selection of resources and solutions.

Minimizing Noise

Priority and time management are optimized when noise is minimized or eliminated. Noise is anything that is irrelevant or that is a distraction from priorities and productivity. Learn to identify what is noise vs. relevant information and tasks.

Evaluate all requests, communications, and information that are coming at you. Control the inflows to be able to stay focused on the strategically important information that is vital to achieving the vision and priorities. Discriminate between what is actionable and what actions *should* be taken. Optimize the resources being used; you are the steward.

Noise is anything that takes your focus off the target. There are many sources of noise such as co-workers, friends, family, news, and gossip. Some of this cannot be avoided but must be managed so you can focus on your priorities to maintain productivity. Effectively managing your work and life balance/integration will help in controlling the noise from personal issues.

Part of noise is the excessive amount of available information, some of which is unnecessary. Information overload can slow down projects. Therefore, it is important to be highly selective in gathering and using information. Eliminate the excess so that the essence of issues is revealed and only the vital and relevant facts, observations, and interpretations are used to craft meaningful strategies. Think of it like reading a professional journal, when reading the abstract is sufficient rather than the entire article.

EXHIBIT 3.3 ■ Advice for Setting Priorities

Advice	Opportunity for Change
Don't take on too much.	Extensive demands can interfere with productivity and quality of work and life. Evaluate your activities, at work and home, to determine their real priority.
Don't become overwhelmed by the sheer number of priorities.	They can't all be priorities. Can some be eliminated, delegated, or delayed? Assess how time and resources are allocated. Ask for more of each, if needed.
Don't try to multitask.	There is no such thing as multitasking; it is actually oscillating your attention rapidly between tasks. Focus on the task at hand to ensure quality before shifting to the next.
Don't rush through a task. Rushing can impact quality and does not allow time for reflection and strategizing.	While at times this may be necessary, a constant rushing can indicate that you are holding on to tasks or work that should be eliminated or delegated.
Don't let noise distract you.	Maintain your focus on identified priorities and tasks that support your vision and mission. Reflect on how time is being spent.
Don't let noise interfere with opportunities to build and sustain relationships.	Recognize the need to spend time with colleagues, team members, and mentors to build relationships and expand learning opportunities. Prioritize family and friends to balance and integrate work and life.

There can be a lot of noise in organizations: chatter, information, and projects that do not add value. Clearly defined priorities that align with the mission and vision will help you decide which projects to tackle and which are noise. Leaders are responsible for ensuring that distractions are minimized within the organization by reducing the bureaucracy, concentrating on priorities, and not adding irrelevant projects. You should also ensure that the drive to minimize noise does not interfere with the relationship building and flow of creativity that are required as part of team building and cohesion. Exhibit 3.3 suggests information for setting priorities.

Being Organized

Being organized is a vital strategy for two reasons: (1) to categorize information for easier access and utilization in making decisions and developing strategies; and (2) to minimize clutter and noise. The latter will help you identify distractions and keep you centered on the priorities and vision. The greater the amount of turbulence, conflict, and ambiguity, the more important being organized will be.

Being organized, whether it pertains to a physical space (like a desk) or your thoughts, is helpful in maximizing efficiency and reducing waste. Much like the "lost keys" that are eventually found on a mountain of "stuff," every expenditure of energy spent waiting, looking, or reworking something is inefficient. Staying organized will minimize these situations.

Strategies for Being Organized

When faced with an overwhelming amount of work, proficient organizing skills are necessary. Being organized will enhance efficiency, thus increasing time for important tasks. It can enable you to easily access needed information or other resources, sort out the urgent from the important, eliminate tasks that are no longer needed, clarify goals, develop new work flows to optimize energy, and break the work into manageable chunks.

Clutter is very dangerous, as it can create an environment where it is difficult to concentrate, pay attention to priorities, and keep track of details. Clutter obscures priorities and interferes with information gathering. Maintain an environment that allows for the continuous viewing of problems, opportunities, and issues. You want ordered systems that will clearly identify what needs to be done and how to access relevant information.

Keep clutter and noise to a minimum. Given the chaotic world in which we live and the many pressing demands, it is vital to keep the mind as free from excess items or worries as possible. Organize your papers, files, and messaging to allow for more precise attention to the issues at hand. Manage how you use communication technologies and social media so they add to the efficiency of your day rather than serve as distracters. Create time and task management mechanics that will help you sort your tasks, schedules, and priorities.

Use checklists to identify all the necessary tasks, ensure they do not conflict, and monitor their progress and completion.

Checklists can be useful to promote safe practices by ensuring that all necessary steps are completed.

Think through how your day is organized to create a disciplined schedule that takes into account how you think and when you are optimally using your time. Schedule the day based on when you are most creative or productive. Periodically look at the structure of how you spend each day. You may find a different routine or schedule that is more accommodating than the one you are currently using.

Periodically, conduct a "pruning" process, like a garage cleaning exercise, to thin out the items that are no longer needed. Cleaning out your office and files, like cleaning out a garage, allows for better utilization of space and assets and can result in quicker access to what you need with less wasted time. The process may result in a new growth of ideas similar to pruning bushes and trees, which encourages fresh, hardy growth to develop.

The importance of being organized increases considerably as workload increases or there are other changes that adversely impact efficiency. Systems that may seem to work well in less demanding situations may not work so well as demands increase. Effective organizing systems must be flexible to meet evolving or emerging needs. Evaluate your processes, utilizing methodologies to identify non-value-added steps, areas of information overload or deficiency, or other organizing elements that are not adding value. Successful organizations utilize processes to continually optimize their value-adding activities and eliminate wasteful actions. Exhibit 3.4 offers more advice for being organized.

Initiative

One can choose to wait for direction and be told what to do, a passive approach, or choose to take the initiative. Taking the initiative is a very positive action. It displays leadership in identifying an issue or opportunity and doing something about it. Effective leaders don't need to be told what to do; they establish or discover direction on their own.

EXHIBIT 3.4 ■ Advice for Being Organized

Advice	Opportunity for Change
Don't wait to get organized.	Stay organized. Your efficiency will be maximized if you stay ahead of the clutter and remain organized in thought and space. Consider your professional and personal processes to determine the value of each activity.
Don't let electronic technology and communication add clutter.	Use social media and e-mail in a manner to add efficiency, not clutter.
Don't rely on memory or ad-hoc organizing systems.	Use checklists, file structures, schedules, and other time and task management tools to remain organized and efficient. Determine the organizing format that works best for your personal style and needs, and then put the format to use.

Ideas frequently come up related to problems or new products and services, but no one is assigned the responsibility to take it on; a discussion may take place, but the idea fizzles out. Initiative is needed in order for the opportunity to become reality. Until someone has the initiative to take some action, nothing happens. The cycle – thought → action → results – requires initiative.

Strategies for Taking the Initiative

Use the visioning of the organization, in whatever forms it has been shared (mission, values, strategic plans, etc.), and identify opportunities to develop creative ideas. Your initiative will be appreciated. You may see an opportunity that is not visible to others. Executives do not have time and energy to tell everyone what to do or to see every opportunity. Taking the initiative is the job of a leader, even if you don't have a formal position of leadership. In a high-performance organization, everyone is tapped for their leadership attributes.

You should demonstrate initiative by solving a problem you've identified. It is easy to identify a problem or raise a complaint, hoping that others will resolve it, but you can show initiative by your willingness to take on the problem and develop a solution. Such initiative will be noted by senior leadership, and they will appreciate and be more receptive to your suggestions.

Initiating a new effort is also a way to deal with boredom that can creep into a job. Every job has some drudgery, paperwork, unexciting details, or repetition. This can actually be an opportunity to innovate a new process or approach that automates or simplifies the work. Develop new approaches for completing those tasks to make them more efficient and effective. This can also free up time so that you can take on another initiative and make your job more interesting. Doing so will also help others recognize the leadership qualities you display.

A lack of initiative can be the result of:

- Not being able to identify issues or new ideas;
- Procrastination or avoidance;
- Not knowing how to solve the problem;
- Indecision; or
- Waiting for the ideal solution...when the best option is not ideal.

Showing lack of initiative can be a career derailer. There is *always* a need to solve problems, develop new solutions, or create new products or services. You must show some initiative in order to demonstrate leadership qualities. You should try to overcome any reasons that may be holding you back.

There may be times when taking the initiative will be negatively perceived by others. You need to be sensitive that they may not see the value or benefit of your idea because it is not part of the business plan, it does not benefit them, or they simply do not understand it. This can be particularly true with ideas diverging from previous products or services or those with benefits in the distant future. Others may reject the idea out of fear that it will mean a loss of prestige and interfere with their own initiatives or out of jealousy that they didn't recognize the opportunity.

This requires a constant vigilance of explaining the opportunity and its benefits and meeting the needs of current stakeholders or leadership. At times it may make sense to wait for the right time, to allow the concept to develop, and to avoid needless anxiety in others. Pushing something at the wrong time is not prudent

EXHIBIT 3.5 ■ Advice for Taking the Initiative

Advice	Opportunity for Change
Don't wait to be told what to do.	If you have an idea or recognize an opportunity, propose it and be prepared to carry it through.
Don't take the initiative without seeking support if you will be changing too much or potentially threatening others.	Recognize when you must seek approval for the idea and prepare your case to elicit support by explaining the benefits.
Don't ignore a new idea because you don't have enough knowledge or time to implement it.	Share your inspiration with others. If they see the possibilities, they can share knowledge or free up some of your time to help you develop it.
Don't be too intense or forceful when trying to generate support for your initiative.	Having a passion and enthusiasm for change efforts is very positive, but if you're perceived as too forceful, some individuals may feel like you are trying to force change. Moderate the intensity level so that others receive it with the intended enthusiasm. There is a difference between being a fan and being *fan*atical.

and may only antagonize others and close their minds to the possibility. Continue to develop the concept, provide supporting evidence on its potential benefits, recognize reasons behind resistance, and practice persuasion until co-workers come around to your idea.

I received recognition for an initiative that I undertook as the first executive vice president of a newly merged medical group practice. I came up with the idea of creating a community foundation to support charitable causes. The idea was met with skepticism, given the number of operational issues related to the merger. I pursued the idea because I strongly believed that our organization should contribute to the community. I was able to overcome the skepticism by partnering with an umbrella community foundation that already existed. We created an account for our contributions and recommended how the distributions would be managed. Over the next several years, we donated considerable dollars to support worthy causes and received recognition by the local chamber of commerce for our efforts. Exhibit 3.5 offers advice for taking the initiative.

Problem Solving

Successful problem solving is more than just solving problems. It is solving them with an eye toward the vision, ensuring that the proposed solution moves the organization closer to its goals. Frequently, immediate solutions are proposed when problems arise. However, care needs to be taken so that choices result in long-term success. Also, it is extraordinarily easy to offer solutions that address the symptoms of problems, not the root cause. This is why it is important to continue asking *why* something occurred. If root causes are not identified, the real problems will repeat or cause issues elsewhere.

Effective problem solving requires a consistent attention to issues with a confidence that the challenges and obstacles will be met and overcome. The following phrase is often stated: There are no problems, just opportunities. Persistent, focused effort will eventually result in success as well as another learning opportunity.

Strategies for Solving Problems

Sample Journal Entry

May 18: It comes to mind that we often respond to problems with solutions in order to feel good that we have done something about the problem. Sometimes we do this to avoid embarrassment or to protect our self-esteem. Oftentimes, this requires changing or establishing processes, or, put more negatively, we establish bureaucracy. At times the solution is worse than the problem. I need to consider the long-term impact of my solutions and changes.

When faced with a problem, organize your thoughts to reduce anxiety and stress. Think through the process first to create a list of issues that will need to be addressed. Then develop some of the questions that need to be answered. You should ask questions to identify the symptoms, effects, influencers, interconnections, patterns, and processes related to the issue. Make sure you identify and address the root cause(s), or else the issue could arise again.

Prior to tackling a problem, you may need to determine if you are the only one that sees it as a problem. Others may have reasons to accept the status quo. In this case, you need to under-stand why they accept it or convince others that there is a prob-lem requiring a resolution. Another option to generate support is to persuade others that your solution will improve the situation to their benefit.

When thinking through problems, assess whether necessary information is available. Never risk the solution and your cred-ibility on inaccurate, incomplete, or outdated information. Determine how the lacking information or knowledge should be obtained.

Some problems or assignments are going to require extensive planning and time. You may even approach an issue with little idea how to solve it. This requires a maturity to develop interim approaches knowing that the plan is going to change once additional information is gathered. Having an end goal (vision) in mind will be important. The strategies and approach may change, but the endgame should not.

Consider the scale of the issue and whether it should be bro-ken down into parts to focus on each element. Frequently, the problem can seem overwhelming when you can't get your arms around it. Solutions and strategies might appear if the problem is broken down into manageable pieces with achievable solutions. You are also more likely to identify more of the issues that need to be addressed. Also, by breaking it down, you can delegate certain aspects to others.

Identify the resources that may be available to identify and implement a solution, including human, financial, and techno-logical resources. Successful problem solving will involve a deep exploration as to how resources can be optimally redeployed and a justification or rationale as to why this makes sense. This includes identifying needed knowledge and skills and the per-sonnel with the complementary competencies. This is critical, as it is not possible to anticipate all problems or issues ahead of time, and teams with the competencies and adaptability are important to adjust to changing circumstances.

Consider possible solutions and strategies to solve the problem. For most issues there are multiple solutions, many of which will provide satisfactory results. You need to find the optimum solution that is long lasting and addresses the core of the problem. Influencing others that your idea for solving the problem will require patience; it may be that you have given a great deal of thought to the proposed solution while others are hearing about it for the first time. Also, consider the benefits of contacting your network or bringing in your high-performing team to collaborate on finding the best solution.

Difficult decisions are challenging and it is easy to vacillate considering the advantages and disadvantages of potential solutions. Too many variables can creep into discussions and create extensive anxiety for all stakeholders. Clarify what the goal is and solicit honest opinions from everyone to craft potential strategies. Decisions will be better with a thoughtful process built on a foundation of a diversity of opinions and trusting relationships.

Also consider possible metrics to help you determine if the chosen answer and implementation strategy are successful. You should measure the results of the solution to track its benefits and to reflect on whether or not the optimal strategy was implemented or if another would have been a better choice.

Solving a problem or completing a task may give the appearance that you can "cross it off the list," but this can provide a false sense of security. The issue is not whether the task was completed as much as the degree of quality or excellence achieved in resolving the issue. Consider the short- and long-term impact of your strategy so that in the future others are not faced with a problem that you created with today's "solution." Exhibit 3.6 addresses more solutions for problem solving.

Change Management

Achieving excellence requires developing a vision, identifying new priorities, and solving problems. Leaders must frequently introduce changes to accomplish these tasks and provide more value to organizations. This is especially true in today's fast-changing environment. Unfortunately, many change efforts fail for a variety of reasons, including:

- Lack of information,
- Resistance to change,

EXHIBIT 3.6 ■ Advice for Solving Problems

Advice	Opportunity for Change
Don't become discouraged by the speed bumps or walls that appear during problem-solving and solution implementation.	This is when leaders get tested. Approach the challenges with a positive mindfulness, drawing on the numerous strategies and resources available to leaders.
Don't be afraid to challenge assumptions.	Others may assume the status quo is okay. Present your reasoning as to why there are solutions or alternatives that are better.
Don't be a fire fighter putting out "fires" that pop up here and there as a result of ineffective planning, strategy, or execution.	Prevent the fires from occurring. Be proactive by contemplating desired long-term results and implementing mechanisms to reduce or prevent problems from developing.
Don't develop tunnel vision by focusing too much on something and losing the context of what is going on in the environment.	It is important to monitor the environment for internal and external changes. What starts out as a good idea can become a bad idea or have unforeseen consequences. Constant surveillance will be helpful to optimize learning and strategy development.
Don't try to solve someone else's problems unless asked.	Know when they need to solve it themselves to build their leadership competency. Be available to coach and provide support that is needed for long-term growth.

- Inertia;
- Lack of a clear vision of the end result;
- Others not seeing the benefits,
- Poor communication,
- Being bogged down in details,
- Losing interest,
- Poor implementation, and
- Lack of adequate resources.

With so many possible reasons, it's no wonder many change efforts don't succeed. All of these elements need to be considered when addressing potential changes. Successful change management requires clear vision, planning, effective implementation strategies, and addressing others' concerns. Effective change management is about doing the right thing, the right way, with the right people, at the right time.

Notice that many of the reasons are related to people. Since it is people that design, implement, and suffer or benefit from the results, change management requires addressing people issues. It requires instilling a desire to change, to move people from the comfortable, through the uncomfortable, to the new reality. Openness to change needs to be part of the organizational culture in today's world of rapid change.

Frequently, there is the belief that resistance is a major factor in failed change efforts. Although this can be factor, it implies a deliberate attempt by others to resist. Another reason to consider is inertia. Implementing changes can require enormous energy, focus, time, and effort. It is easier to maintain the status quo than to consider each of the systems and processes that will be involved in the change.

Strategies for Change Management

Leading large, complex change requires considerable capability. A successful change leader is:

- Positive...optimistic with inspiring motivations;
- Patient...compassionate and gives time for people to adjust; and
- Persistent...fights inertia and overcomes resistance.

When preparing to initiate change, think through the short- and long-range implications of the actions you are about to take. Are the actions likely to move you closer or further away from the vision? What are the possible consequences of the action, including the big or small, immediate or gradual, short-term or long-term effects? Remember, your actions may begin a cascade of other reactions. You don't want to be surprised by any unexpected consequences.

Initiate the change by presenting reasons for it, why inertia must be overcome and people must move from current habits to the unknown. Clearly state the desired end result and expected benefits. Demonstrate how the change will align with the organizational vision or address a particular problem.

When contemplating a change, prepare to commit to the planning and coordination efforts, particularly if it will be a large-scale or significant change. Develop tactics to implement the change and assign individuals tasks with specific goals and timelines. Anticipate potential issues and consequences that might develop as well as possible strategies for managing them. Thorough planning can mean the difference between being proactive vs. having to fight "fires" – to address the many problems that can pop up.

Change management efforts will be much more effective if more time and effort is spent up front to "charter" the change to identify the mission, goals, scope, involved individuals, tasks, and so on. This does not need to be overly complicated or bureaucratic, but it must be a transparent clarification with consensus on the purpose of the effort and assigned tasks. Use visual cues to keep others on track, like whiteboards, posters, metrics, and so forth. Consider including comments about possible positive or negative environmental factors that may develop in the future which could significantly influence the change effort.

Influencing change in large, complex organizations can be challenging. One effective strategy is to break the issues into parts that are more manageable. Successful completion of each part or project will result in a sense of achievement and progress toward the total goal. However, groups and teams need to be brought together to coordinate and understand the global goal. If you don't bring everyone together, then there is an increased opportunity for miscommunication, missed information, or for each task to be conducted in a silo based on narrower goals and interests. Bringing them together will allow for sharing common issues, solutions, and concerns.

Effective change management will consider facts, assumptions, biases, prejudices, and both environmental and political forces. Take the time to step back and consider all of the potential influences. Ask questions about options, strategies, concerns, feelings, and so forth to understand any reservations or objections of the planned change. Not asking questions can result in faulty assumptions or interpretations. Also consider any possible roadblocks or delays and identify their potential workarounds.

Change and Others

Consider how various stakeholders will be impacted from the change by placing yourself in their shoes. Individuals will probably not accept your ideas as is. They will need a rationale and explained benefit to accept the change. Influencing change is about attending to the needs and desires of others. Showing sensitivity and compassion for those impacted by the change will go a long way in building relationships. You must respond with an enthusiastic and positive effect.

Change efforts come with a variety of stressors, some small and some huge, and may generate intense emotional reactions. Some individuals will respond negatively with potential reactions including cynicism, frustration, fear, stress, and resistance. Recognize that it is typical for others to pass through emotional transitions, including disengagement and disorientation, which will result in different thinking and behavior. You need to consider each of these potential reactions and emotions in helping others manage the change. This is one of the reasons why change management is difficult.

One option for overcoming resistance is to build a coalition of change agents. Identify individuals in the organization who support the change. Let them help you identify reasons for and options to overcome the resistance and encourage them to present the case for change to others. If your agents are from a variety of departments, they can also serve as representatives between the department and the planners. For example, in healthcare organizations, identifying several physicians or other stakeholders to support your change will ease the transition if they present the case to other physicians and help them overcome their reasons for resistance.

When leading (changing) others, consider process, emotions, optimism, logic, and creativity when thinking through issues. People have different values (what is important to them), and they live their values by having a different focus on what is important. An effective negotiating strategy is to understand their values and utilize their language. This will make it easier for them to understand and connect with the change process.

Focusing on one or a few initiatives with high potential payoffs can result in a lot of support and integrated effort. If there are many changes, "an initiative of the month," people can lose interest and integrity can be damaged. If there is divided or little focus, there may be a tendency to provide lackluster support or just wait out an initiative, knowing that "this too shall pass."

Consider who the sponsor or communicator of the change is. Employees expect information and communication from certain individuals, whether those with a certain professional back-ground (i.e., physicians) or level of authority in the organization (i.e., executive or physician partner). Consider who is delivering the news, as this will profoundly impact the results. For exam-ple, if the communicator is senior leadership, employees will be impressed with the importance of the change and organizational commitment.

Effective change management is also going to depend on your formal and informal role. If you suggest change that is not within your realm of influence, your suggestion may not be accepted positively despite your best intentions. Your recommen-dations may also cause damage to relationships. Before offering opinions, consider how your idea will be perceived or establish that your views are wanted.

The ultimate test of a change initiative is whether the desired results are achieved. Part of the change process is to identify metrics to track results, ensuring there is sustainable value. Monitor the outcome to confirm that others do not revert to the old system or find ways to game the system, resulting in unin-tended consequences. Exhibit 3.7 lists more recommendations for change management.

Achieving Results

There can be a tendency or enthusiasm to discuss ideas, but follow-through and results are frequently not achieved. This can be due to changing conditions, lack of persistence, or lack of accountability. Life frequently gets in the way or priorities are shifted. However, results must be achieved to meet organiza-tional goals and the vision, and to remain competitive. Leaders

EXHIBIT 3.7 ■ Advice for Change Management

Advice	Opportunity for Change
Don't underappreciate the complexity of the change or fail to consider all of the factors.	Take the time to scope out issues with the appropriate amount of project planning.
Don't overpromise and underdeliver.	Maintain your credibility by preparing an accurate timeline and assessment of the impact and benefits of the change.
Do not try to implement too many changes at one time. This may increase the anxiety and confusion.	Initiate one major change at a time. Allow people time to adjust to one change before another is started.
Don't be an alarmist when advocating for change. Being an alarmist will reduce your credibility and might actually have the opposite effect.	It is better to build a case for rational change around visions, goals, strategies, values, and benefits rather than to appeal to someone only through emotions.
Don't be callous or insensitive to others' feelings.	Change can be very emotional for others, involving grief, loss, and fear. Successful change efforts are going to be more lasting and positive if you are sensitive to their concerns and the transitions they may need to go through.
Do not proceed without obtaining buy-in. What may appear as a good, rapid decision could be an illusion.	Ensure there is a high level of commitment. Proceed with caution, patience, and persistence.
Don't evaluate the impact and results of the change too early.	Wait until the potential negative emotions have dissipated and people have become adjusted to the change.

are judged by their ability to see initiatives through to completion and to demonstrate results.

Many individuals have a lot of opinions and ideas, but not all take the initiative and develop the resources, skills, and relationships to implement them. Then there are the few individuals who go beyond the expected, to achieve results that could not even have been imagined; these are the ultimate *results-oriented* leaders.

Some results will come quickly and fairly easily, whereas others take more time and planning. The long-term resolution of problems may take considerably more effort, discipline, time, and patience. This is where leadership excellence gets tested.

Strategies for Achieving Results

Being results oriented means focusing your time, energy, resources, and attention on the desired outcome. However, achieving results will also depend on your authority, competency, assertiveness, accountability, and persistence. You are more likely to succeed if you have clear goals, conduct thorough planning, specify key deliverables, identify the correct individuals to be team members, develop successful implementation strategies, identify metrics of success, and persist to project completion.

Being results oriented is contextual. You may get good results, but if the outcome is not what is expected or valued by others, then the results will not be appreciated. Thus, it is important to align activities around the desires and needs of leadership and the organization.

Achieving results is not synonymous with being busy. There are an infinite number of ways to waste time and energy or to spend time on low value-added activities. Being incredibly efficient doing the wrong thing will not end with positive results; you will just get to the wrong place faster. Conduct frequent assessments to evaluate whether efforts are aligned with organizational priorities and will result in the expected and desired benefits. This assessment will be more effective if it is done in an atmosphere of openness and without looking for blame or shame.

The key to achieving valued results is having a defined goal aligned with organizational priorities and the vision. Goals serve as a magnet, to focus time and energy toward a specific objective. Inspirational goals are more likely to attract and gain the commitment of others. Write down the goal to ensure it is clear, explicitly stated, and with defined outcomes. Share it with your team and review it regularly to generate more reflection and attention. Be open to modifying the strategies if needed to maintain your commitment to achieving the goal and obtaining needed results.

To achieve the desired results, study the issue and goal to identify appropriate solutions, strategies, and resources. Use your project management skills to align purpose, roles, timelines, and metrics. Timelines with specific completion dates and assigned tasks will help establish accountability and commitment from others. Establishing dates will inspire a deeper reflection on how to marshal the attention and resources needed to comply with the project schedule.

As the project proceeds, measure progress and interim results, provide feedback, and be ready to adapt strategies as needed. Look for opportunities to improve processes and results by implementing new strategies, new processes, new approaches, or developing new management or team talent. Consider having a periodic review conducted by someone outside the work unit, such as an auditor or other individual with expert knowledge of the business. This objectivity will help you avoid groupthink or a loss of perspective and could generate new ideas.

Another strategy is to look at the structure of the organization or unit. At times, the roles and responsibilities of team members are not optimally designed or clearly identified or communicated. This can lead to a tendency to work harder but often masks the ineffective or inefficient processes or lack of appropriate skills or knowledge. Evaluate the processes and team member roles to identify potential improvements and minimize waste.

Achieving desired results is easier with enablers, strategies, mechanisms, and tools that provide automated guides or prompts for maintaining focus on the desired behavior. For example, a weekly planner for work and life can coordinate activities, and whiteboards can list department employees and their accountabilities. Combine these approaches with procedural, design, and process guides to stay focused and achieve the desired results. You should consider using project management tools for managing time and initiatives at work.

Remember that achieving results requires taking the long view and a patience that progress comes slowly, especially on complex projects. Ensure the completion of each step, each task. A good analogy is professional football and the goal of winning the Super Bowl. Winning the big game is accomplished by winning other games. Games are won by scoring touchdowns, and touchdowns are completed by reaching first downs. You can have all of the "trick plays" you want, but you must still control the ball and keep getting first downs.

There is a natural tendency to continue to use strategies that have been successful in the past; why change if they have worked before? However, you will be more successful if you consider the unique characteristics of the current situation and team members, and are willing to adapt tactics as needed. Unlike the phrase, "if at first you don't succeed, try harder," perhaps a better strategy is "if at first you don't succeed, try something different."

When results are not satisfactory, consider which factors may be interfering with success. You could be affected by negative variables such as worry, constant reprioritization, wasted effort, ineffective meetings, ineffective use of technology, waiting for others, not having clear goals, ineffective processes, or poor relationships. Identify the means or seek help to overcome these obstacles.

Achieving results is the best strategy for secure employment. For example, when I was between jobs years ago, I rewrote my resume to identify the accomplishments I had achieved and the results I had obtained. I knew that recruiters would be more interested in me if I demonstrated my ability to achieve desired results.

There are several strategies that you can use to demonstrate you are results oriented. Be known as the individual who gets the projects done and achieves excellent results. Volunteer, reach out, and identify ways that you can contribute. Other strategies include:

- Document accomplishments;
- Work on high-priority/visible projects;
- Maintain a visible and active involvement;
- Tackle difficult problems;
- Be accountable to timelines and metrics; and
- Regularly communicate with leadership on project status and to maintain alignment.

In previous chapters, I've described several characteristics that will contribute to being results oriented, including having vision, setting priorities, and being organized. Additional characteristics include being accountable and being persistent.

Accountability

Obtaining results requires leaders to be accountable and to hold others accountable. Being accountable means taking on an initiative, role, or assignment and being committed to completing it with the desired outcomes. It means accepting responsibility for those under you and holding them accountable for their assignments.

Establishing accountability will help others manage their energy more effectively. It is important to be assertive, specific in defining their responsibilities and timelines, and ensuring they understand and are committed to completing their assignments. When holding others accountable to complete assignments, ensure they share the same priorities and inspiring vision and have the needed competencies.

Holding others accountable is much more difficult in VUCA (volatile, uncertain, complex, and ambiguous) situations, a concept that comes from the military. Today's healthcare environment is frequently similar when facing internal and external changes in uncertain and complex times. Even in these chaotic situations, accountability needs to be specified, so that nothing falls through the cracks, but with the flexibility to adjust to changing circumstances. Achieving excellence and maintaining accountability in this environment requires exceptional leadership.

Persistence

Persistence is continuing to pursue strategies and goals despite obstacles. It is about staying focused and resilient despite setbacks, and having the discipline to push on to achieve results despite a desire to give up. Strategic organizational issues or challenges will frequently require the most persistence and discipline since the payoff may be more difficult and more distant.

Persistence is vital to ensure that strategies are developed to implement the idea or change and to hold others accountable for their assigned tasks. It is also about adjusting strategies to incorporate changing or emerging issues and conducting follow-up to ensure that desired results are achieved. This means following through on projects, discussions, ideas, initiatives, and others' commitments. Follow-up should include mechanisms to track and ensure that assignments are completed as planned and

EXHIBIT 3.8 ■ Advice for Achieving Results

Advice	Opportunity for Change
Don't let distractions interfere with achieving results.	Results are achieved by disciplined strategy, focus, and execution. Slow down to assess whether distractions are getting in the way of achieving results.
Don't get caught up in less-valued goals or results.	Ensure that desired outcomes are aligned with organizational priorities and vision.
Don't seek results for glory. There is no need to look for or expect recognition.	Focus on results for the sole purpose of helping the organization and customers. Leaders are expected and need to produce results.
Don't become so results oriented that you lose sight of relationships.	Take a pulse check on whether you have a balance between task vs. people orientation. You need both for long-term success. Recognize others for their contributions.
Don't show lack of assertiveness when holding others accountable.	Holding others accountable can be uncomfortable and you may cause anger. If you don't enforce accountability, significant long-term issues can appear, including losing team commitment and trust in your abilities.
Don't take the easy way out by ignoring a task, giving up, or blaming others when faced with difficult situations.	Be committed to finishing the assigned project or your initiative. Try another approach, strategy, or seek advice from your network/team.
Don't lose confidence when the envisioned result is not achieved.	Conduct a mindful reflection or after-action review to identify the cause of the poor result and what can be done better. Learn from the experience.

on time. Avoid situations where results were not achieved simply because of a lack of follow-up.

Your persistence will be tested in circumstances that appear somewhat hopeless or when you don't know which way to turn. This is a sensitive time because counterproductive options exist to avoid or delay the assignment. Commit to finish the task by working through the challenges or developing different strategies or approaches. Focus on incremental improvements to support the final vision. Continue to push through until desired results are obtained. Exhibit 3.8 offers advice for achieving results.

EXHIBIT 3.9 ■ Questions for Reflection: Leading Organizations

Excellence:	What strategies do you use to achieve or maintain excellence?
	Do you reflect and learn from past decisions and mistakes?
	How do you help others achieve excellence?
Vision:	What strategies do you use to inspire others?
	How do you communicate a compelling vision?
Priorities:	What strategy has been most effective for you as a leader in maintaining alignment?
	What strategy have you used effectively in balancing the short- and long-term concerns in making decisions?
Being Organized:	How do you eliminate wasted energy and time?
	Do you routinely review your daily life activities to optimize effectiveness and efficiency, and eliminate wasted effort?
Initiative:	How are individuals in your organization encouraged to take initiative?
	What strategies do you use to overcome resistance to an initiative?
Problem Solving:	Do you view problems as stressors or opportunities?
	How do you identify the root cause before tackling a problem?
	What strategies do you use to address problems in a positive, patient, and persistent manner?
Change Management:	What strategies do you use to facilitate complex change efforts?
	How do you motivate others to change, and are you sensitive to their emotions?
Achieving Results:	What mechanisms do you use to ensure that results are achieved?
	How do you avoid distractions or mixed messages and focus on results?

Action items: What two or three specific actions will you commit to as a result of reading this chapter on Leading Organizations by Achieving Excellence?

1. _____

2. _____

3. _____

Conclusion

The third part of the leadership model (after leading self and others) is to lead organizations with the goal of achieving excellence, whether you have a formal leadership position or not. The high-performing and standard-setting organizations that will thrive will help everyone contribute as a leader. Achieving organizational excellence relies on your abilities as a leader to help others achieve excellence through their efforts. The questions in Exhibit 3.9 will help you reflect on your capability to achieve excellence and help your organization excel.

CHAPTER FOUR

Work–Life Integration and Synergy

Integrated Leadership Model

Leading Others:
Developing Relationships

- Professionalism
- Listening
- Conflict
- Assertiveness
- Diversity and Inclusiveness
- Perspective

Leading Self:
Through Learning

- Reflection
- Humility
- Frustration, Anger, Anxiety
- Optimism and Patience
- Resilience and Confidence

Work-Life Integration and Synergy

Leading Organizations:
Achieving Excellence

- Vision
- Priorities and Being Organized
- Initiative
- Problem Solving
- Change Management
- Achieving Results

©2013 Ronald Menaker

Achieving Sustainable Success and Satisfaction

Why is it important to consider work–life integration and synergy to achieve sustainable success and satisfaction as a leader? Integration and synergy definitions provide some guidance. *Integration* can be defined as "an act of combining into an integral whole" or as "behavior that is in harmony with the environment" (Dictionary.com). *Synergy* can be defined as "the interaction of elements that when combined produce a greater total effect, a cooperative action" (Dictionary.com). Success and satisfaction in work *and* life are more likely to be achieved when there is a balance in *both*. If demands in one are greater than can be effectively managed, the other will probably suffer.

Many individuals think it is sufficient to concentrate on leading others or the organization to become a successful leader. However, work–life integration is where many leaders get derailed and it is a necessary part of leading self. Achieving momentary success can happen regularly. The challenge is to have excellence/success replicated continuously, whatever the situation. There needs to be recognition and appreciation that success can't be at the expense of individual health or relationships with others, or else burnout can occur. An effective leader, in addition to leading self, others, and organizations, will need to incorporate strategies on work–life balance, integration, and synergy, so that personal and professional satisfaction and success are sustainable for the long term.

Striving for excellence has a strong upside, but there is a downside as well, when it requires more of your time and others place even more demands on you than are sustainable. Poor work–life balance can be a frequent and undesirable by-product of a continual approach to doing more. Maintaining a healthy work–life balance and integration is an extraordinarily complex task because of the competing values and demands on your time by you and others.

There are an endless number of activities, chores, opportunities, needs, and interests, both at work and outside of work. Americans also have a tendency to do things in excess: more work, more interests, more family activities, and so on. Too much of anything can be toxic in the long term, even if it is beneficial if used or present in the right quantity. For example, eating too much food leads to obesity and consuming too many vitamins can lead to toxicity. In particular, excessive work can cause other aspects of life (family, friends, health, etc.) to suffer. Burnout is a very real threat when faced with too many demands and when an imbalance exists in work and life.

Work–life integration is an important leadership concept and can only be achieved by a mindful discipline. Aristotle, the

Greek philosopher, spoke of virtues representing the midpoint between excess and deficiency. When considering all actions, consider whether you are approaching an excess or deficiency. Avoiding extremes is more likely going to optimize the results.

Achieving a healthy balance requires discipline to say no to further commitments. Successful work–life balance is finding the "sweet spot" of doing what you want to do, what you have to do, and what others want you to do. Too much focus on only one of these factors can adversely impact results. Finding the right equilibrium can result in both happiness *and* success. Discover the right balance for you by considering all aspects of life: family, work, profession, recreation, friends, health, spirituality, and community. Think of each of these values as spokes on a wheel; the "wheel" of life will not run smoothly if any spoke is out of alignment.

Achieving work–life balance is enhanced with a continuous replenishment of energy: physically, emotionally, socially, and spiritually. Each source of energy addresses important needs we all have. The key is maintaining a balance between energy demands (work, chores, etc.) and energy sources.

Strategies for Work–Life Balance and Integration

Given the extensive challenges in healthcare, it is clear that the potential for overwork is very real. This is especially true in stressful positions with the increasing amounts of work and pressure accumulating from time to time. You need to be sensitive to increasing and unrealistic amounts of work since no one else will know about all of the demands on your time. As you achieve excellence and more success, you likely will be given more work and responsibilities. You will need to manage your work–life balance by monitoring and controlling your workload and deciding when there is too much demand.

Frequently, stress is the result of having many responsibilities and a wide variety of interests. Ironically, much of the stress can be the result of trying to do too many desirable activities that if done by themselves would not be an issue but collectively are too much to enjoy. Stress is all self-imposed by the choices we make and our reaction to the stressors. Several ways to control reaction to stress have already been described, including patience, optimism, and maintaining resiliency and perspective. Additional strategies for making choices and maintaining a work–life balance/integration include:

- Reflection;
- Determining values and priorities;
- Organizing and time management;
- Choosing the correct job or career;
- Relaxation and recreation;
- Balancing financial interests; and
- Accepting reality.

Reflection

Work–life balance is constantly in need of calibration. The pressures of day to day can become overwhelming, with too many demands placed on you. Although you can work more hours, you can't commit more than 100 percent of your total available energy. If you work more hours, something else is reduced, including time for yourself or your family. Just as reflection is an important tool in managing self at work, it is also crucial to slow down to reflect on your health, your total workload, and your personal priorities.

Chaos can seem like the reality of life, at times. During periods of chaos, slow down to reflect using whatever mechanism works for you (meditating, running, journalizing, etc.). Reflection is one mechanism to return meaning back into the chaos, to look for the patterns that are creating the cause and effect. Use reflection as a step toward creating a new, less-chaotic reality. Use the opportunity to evaluate what conditions are present that are causing a poor match between the work and life demands. Is it a lack of resources, ineffective or inefficient execution, or too many demands?

Oftentimes, your accomplishments come very slowly and may not be perceived or may be forgotten. Moving too fast can cause a loss of perspective. Also, you are more likely to react to what is immediately around you, not recognizing that the current situation is temporary or other reactions are needed. If reflection is not occurring, moments of emotional exhaustion may become more common, as will negative or inappropriate emotions. Slowing down will help you appreciate what is happening, what is going well, and to reflect on the positive results that have been achieved; this will help place the negative in perspective.

Work–life balance may require a periodic refresher. Most religions have times during the year to reflect, whether it is the "new year" or some other time of contemplation. Periods of transitions, such as changes in your employment situation, also provide an opportunity to reflect. This practice is healthy since it provides an opportunity to reflect on the past and the current, and to consider a better future for you and others. This reflection can provide an emotional, analytical, and spiritual cleansing. The time should be used to reassess, reprioritize, recalibrate, develop new hobbies and habits, eliminate bad habits, develop new competencies, or prepare for the future.

Determining Values and Priorities

Work–life balance requires an accurate understanding of your values, goals, priorities, and strategies for time management. There are an infinite number of options to consider in life and you are faced with constant choices involving demands for your time, selection of projects, and career choices. Decisions are frequently made without considering your strategic life goals or the impact of some decisions on others. There are many variables to consider; the unplanned life can become a mindless display of habits that are unfocused and without direction.

The key is to determine your values; *write them down*. For each of these values, establish a vision of what your desired state is and then determine your priorities to achieve that vision. Next, write an explicit mission statement that describes your purpose and reason for living, such as "to love and care for myself, family, and friends." There is no right or wrong with regard to your personal mission/vision/value statements; the purpose is to clearly articulate what you want out of life. This will make it easier for you to be mindful and faithful to decisions and actions that bring these statements to life.

Using your values, vision, and mission statement, determine the priorities in your life and identify the strategies to balance them. Developing a strategic plan for your "integrated" life and career will help you evaluate the choices available to you and how you balance life choices to achieve synergy. Include an assessment of your SWOT. Consider your current job, career goals, professional activities, family, friends, hobbies/interests, and community activities.

During these times of reflection and consideration, it is critical to place the highest level of focus on maintaining health. This is the most fundamental of priorities and the easiest to forget and place at a lower priority. Poor health can have devastating consequences to work, life, and family. There can be no true wealth, however it is calculated, without true health.

In home and career, you can now use your vision and goals when faced with opportunities and choices to determine which option will either move you closer to or further away from your plan. Some of these choices may be seductive, such as receiving a promotion, working for a different organization, or making more money. Be mindful about the long-term impact of the options. At times you may have to sacrifice the short term for the long term. Make wise choices...you don't want to look back at your life, in regret, as a misdirection in effort or poor choices.

Organizing and Time Management

Use your strategic plan and list of priorities to focus your time, effort, and energy and to identify the noise or distractions that could cause interference. In life, practice several of the time management techniques that are recommended for demands at work, including:

- Focusing on priorities;
- Eliminating waste and distractions;
- Delegating; and
- Utilizing time management tools.

When you have established a vision, identify ways to focus your energy on your priorities. Design your work flows to build in mechanisms to reinforce these activities by considering what should be built in, automatically. Activities that you want to have happen regularly may include time with the family or friends and activities to maintain a healthy lifestyle. Use the schedule to identify daily, weekly, monthly, and annual cycles that will optimize your efforts and commit you to your vision. Accept that the schedule must remain flexible, but the focus on priorities must continue.

You should consider which activities – and, therefore, commitment of time and energy – are a choice and which are a priority. Frequently, the choices are looked at in isolation, but each decision has short-term results leading to long-term cumulative consequences. Committing to too many choices may result in competing priorities, exhaustion, and the proclamation that "I don't have enough time." Evaluate all of the choices to determine which are priorities and which can be eliminated. Identify the distractions that will demand your time and energy but divert you from your priorities. Practice lean principles in your nonwork life in order to eliminate waste, duplication, waiting times, reprocessing, clutter, and other value-reducing activities.

Achieving work–life balance is not just about what is being done, but who is doing the work. Not everything needs to be done by you. Although cutting the lawn may provide some exercise and washing the windows yourself can save you some money, these activities may not be the best use of your time. Trying to "do it all" is not likely to optimize results. There are many options to reduce your effort on less important tasks in order to provide much needed time for your higher priorities. Consider delegating projects to others in the family or to contractors.

Many tools are available to optimize your time management and improve work–life balance. Almost all activities utilize some type of method or technology, whether involving communications (cellular phone, iPad, pager, etc.), organization systems (file folders), or other technologies employed in work or home projects. Reflect on whether your toolbox includes the most helpful, appropriate tools. Determine if you are using an outdated method to complete your work. This can be easy to forget as we cling to old habits, even when they are no longer efficient. Slight changes in process can be very important to address the increasing demands on your time.

Choosing the Correct Job or Career

There will be times in any job when it is boring, stressful, or no longer enjoyable. However, there are times when this is a sign that you are in the wrong role, with the wrong organization, or in the wrong industry. If you are in a job or career that you do not enjoy, one that does not consider your talents, interests, or needs, then you may try to attain work–life balance through recreation, hobbies, and other non-work-related activities. If you are not enjoying your job, if it is a chore, ask yourself why you are doing it.

True work–life balance is harmony on the job and at home. If you are employed in a position that is in line with your passion, interests, and talents, then efforts to achieve work–life balance may be less focused on escaping work. You will focus more energy on professional activities because it brings a natural enjoyment. You will be more willing to commit time and effort on professional activities and the hours of learning to achieve excellence in your career.

Find a position or career that *synergizes* your talents, training, interests, and experiences. Join an organization with a culture that aligns with your values and personality. Choose an occupation that is intrinsically rewarding and will sustain you in the long term. Successful work–life balance will be improved when you are in a position or career that maximizes success (considering your talents and competencies), happiness (considering your interests, values, and goals), and your tolerance for stress (considering your emotional intelligence and personality).

Relaxation and Recreation

Your effectiveness as a leader will be impacted by the *"re's"*: the extent that you *re*lax, *re*flect, *re*new, and *re*create. These are not luxuries *if* you have the time. They are investments in yourself and your ability to maintain resilience and sustainability.

Part of the "balancing" process is taking time off to recreate. It is important to take some time off to be with family, to engage in healthy behaviors, and to devote time to hobbies, learning, and/or complementary skill development. Taking some time off will encourage others to follow your lead by demonstrating the cultural expectation that all work is not healthy and must be balanced.

Recreation is critical for long-term success; it offers an opportunity to refresh and replenish expended energy. You should not feel guilty about taking time to relax; this also requires discipline. More is not always better and, in fact, can be the cause of harm or significant wasted time and resources. You must have some time for rest. This is not necessarily being idle, but some forms of relaxation are necessary for achieving the vision and committing to the long term. Pacing and balance are critical considerations. Being mindful of these dynamics is an important strategy to achieve long-term work–life balance.

A healthy work–life pace needs to be established in order to have long-term effectiveness and sustainability. Using the word *patience* as a foundation, take the first two and last two letters of the word…it spells *pace*. The combination of patience and a healthy pace are needed to effectively complete complex projects and to be ready for the next. Having a hard-driving personality may obtain short-term results, but may make it difficult to go the distance with healthy relationships and results. Consider the strategy of completing a marathon: setting too fast a pace may lead to exhaustion before the end of the race. The key is to maintain a *sustainable* pace to keep from wearing out prematurely.

Balancing Financial Interests

Many people seek careers or jobs only because of the potential income. However, there are several factors you should consider before you prioritize money. Your salary is usually a function of three things: your employer's need to fill the position, your ability to do the job, and the employer's ease of replacing you with someone else. When considering a plan for life, it is critical to consider all three of these factors, not just the actual dollars. You are more likely to have sustainable employment in a career in which you have a greater ability than other individuals, and your ability is more likely to develop if you enjoy what you are doing.

While you need to determine your highest priorities (values), consider placing money toward the bottom of the list. Think of money as being the result of doing other things well, such as following your vision, learning, being persistent, and finding your passion. Money has been described as being something that won't make you happy once you have enough of it. There can be a temptation to continue to want more, as it oftentimes is an "indicator" of success.

Although the idea of salary normally conjures up images of money and what income you would like, think about "salary" in a broader concept by incorporating the idea of psychic income. Psychic income relates to the happiness and satisfaction that you receive from your job, along with the value that you contribute to society. The psychic income may bring you more personal "wealth" than your salary.

When seeking a healthy work–life balance, consider the lifestyle you are seeking. Be mindful of what makes you happy and that you don't depend on acquiring assets to find happiness. Having too many financial obligations may result in you staying in a job that will not provide you with success or happiness. This is a personal and professional choice but you must accept reality. You cannot maintain a lifestyle that is greater than your salary, and you will not earn more salary just because you want a more expensive lifestyle. Evaluate your needs and desires to determine the lifestyle and expenditure choices that are actually *needed* vs. those that are *wanted* but you can live without.

Find the right balance between living within your income, enjoying some of life's pleasures, and saving for the unexpected. While saving for a "rainy day" is admirable and necessary, being miserly and denying satisfaction to yourself and family is not desirable. Money is only useful if it provides for the needs and desires of you and others. Don't save so much that you are denying yourself some pleasures.

Accepting Reality

Life can be full of happiness and success, but it can also be full of sadness and failure. To only accept the former is not displaying much leadership. The reality is that life is messy and that bad or unexpected things happen. In fact, it is during the tough times that leaders are most needed by others. You need to be ready for the inevitable bumps in the road; some of them will be severe. This is the opportunity for leaders to be a model of leadership behavior for others, both colleagues and family, especially when there is massive pressure or disappointment.

If you want the gain, you need to handle the pain. A rose comes with thorns. Rain will result in rainbows and new growth. Each of these statements is drawing attention to the reality of life. There are going to be challenging stressors, mistakes, and setbacks. Be prepared to rise to the challenge, working harder to achieve the desired results, and finding ways to deal with the setbacks. It is your response to these circumstances that must be managed, and this is where the art of leadership is demonstrated.

The reality of football is that many passes are dropped and some will be intercepted. The reality of baseball is that many swings at the plate result in strikes and only a few in home runs. The reality of life is that rewards come with risks. To run from the risks guarantees no rewards. To punish yourself or others when mistakes are made or rewards are delayed is punitive and will guarantee a more cautious approach and may create a vicious cycle of mediocrity. Don't make this your reality of leadership. This is when the professionalism kicks in, to inspire and motivate for future success.

Prudence will help you consider that the unexpected is bound to happen. Various types of insurance (health, car, home, etc.) were created for these events. Similarly, it is prudent to have mechanisms in place to prepare for downturns and to provide protection during life, especially when attempting new, complicated, or dangerous efforts. For example, mountain climbers use ropes and they train for all types of treacherous conditions, or else they risk injury or death.

Prudence is having outlines of contingency plans for how you will respond when bad things happen, if you lost your job, for example. Go through the "what if" exercise or what you would do if you were asked for your letter of resignation tomorrow. Are you prepared for this? Are you marketable? Is your network in place? How will you adjust your life if you are out of work for an extended period of time? Do you have a financial safety net to help you prepare for these types of potential situations? The time to prepare for such situations is when all is going well. Exhibit 4.1 suggests ideas for achieving work–life integration and synergy.

EXHIBIT 4.1 ■ Advice for Achieving Work–Life Integration and Synergy

Advice	Opportunity for Change
Don't let yourself become over-committed to the point that projects, relationships, health, and results are impacted.	Be mindful of a growing number of competing needs. Commit time and energy to your priorities, and minimize the distractions.
Don't let yourself get exhausted.	Exhaustion is a huge red flag that you are out of balance, that you are sacrificing your health. Develop strategies to identify earlier warning signs that you have upset the balance and need to reprioritize, reorganize, and recreate. Rebalance to maintain a sustainable work–life integration and synergy.
Don't become a victim of excess or vices in your work and life. Don't become addicted to overworking, smoking, drugs, drinking alcohol, or overeating.	It is not reasonable to be perfect in life, but you do need to think through your choices; there are adverse impacts of excess in virtually anything. Be mindful of the longer-term impact of living as you are and ask if this is consistent with your values, vision, and strategies. Addictions and excess can be a sign of emotional imbalance; seek help to restore balance.
Don't let yourself be too serious.	Personal joy is a desirable result as it becomes the fuel or energy for future success. As with most efforts and strategies, too much seriousness can be detrimental.
Don't lose sight of reality.	Mistakes occur, wrong turns are taken, and bad things happen. This is part of life. Maintain your perspective, a positive orientation, composure, and a focus on excellence; these are the marks of a leader.
Don't confuse *needs* and *wants*.	Reorient your life to prioritize what you *need*; *wants* may be desirable, but not receiving them won't be as detrimental. This orientation may also result in more altruism by recognizing that there are others who don't have their needs met.

EXHIBIT 4.2 ■ Questions for Reflection on Work–Life Integration and Synergy

- Do you have a strategic plan for your life, incorporating your mission, vision, values, and talents?
- Do you systematically review your values and priorities, incorporating the natural transitions of life?
- How do you maintain resilience and work–life integration while juggling competing demands on your time?
- How do you relax, recreate, and refresh?

Action items: What two or three specific actions will you commit to as a result of reading this chapter on Work–Life Integration and Synergy?

1. _____

2. _____

3. _____

Conclusion

The fourth part of the leadership model, in the center of the model, is work–life integration. Without this integration and balance, being able to maintain success in the other three areas – leading self, others, and organizations – can suffer. The questions in Exhibit 4.2 will help you reflect on your capability to maintain a balance of work and life in order to achieve long-term sustainable success and satisfaction.

CHAPTER FIVE

Leadership...The Journey

Leadership is a journey that begins in school and continues throughout life. Each new assignment, position, or challenge offers an opportunity to learn from experiences, both good and bad, and from others. From these opportunities, competencies and strategies are developed that will help you achieve personal excellence and help others and organizations strive for and achieve success.

My 37-year career, mostly in healthcare organizations, has provided me with many rich opportunities to learn, reflect, and cultivate practical strategies to improve and apply leadership practices. Journalizing during these years has been one of my tools in the process, serving as an aide to reflect and learn from the many challenges, observations, and inspirations. Journal entries also provided a location to record and reread leader- ship observations. Some of the observations, which could also be called "notes or memos to self," are quick reminders of the priorities and keys to achieving long-term personal and orga- nizational success while maintaining work–life integration and balance.

Over time, I have realized there is an integrated leadership model that incorporates the concepts of leading self, others, and orga- nizations to achieve excellence; it relies on the integration of work and life in order to maintain long-term success. I identified writing this book as a means of sharing this model with others.

Leading Self...Be Positive, Patient, Persistent

My "memo to self" to be positive, patient, and persistent has been the overarching message for self-leadership. Taking away any of these elements reduces effectiveness in self-management or in enhancing relationships with others. Successful change efforts require all three elements. Also, I've learned that attitudes are contagious; if you practice these characteristics, others around you are more apt to adopt them.

To lead self, focus your attention on what needs to be studied and learned. We learn in three ways: by reading, through experience, and from interacting with others. Read, read, and read some more about your work and life priorities in order to approach the thousands of hours of learning and practice required to become an expert. Learn about yourself and how to develop your leadership competencies and characteristics so that others will perceive you as a leader to follow. Reflect on your experiences, both good and bad, and what can be learned from each.

Be mindful of the affect that you emote. Emphasize humility, optimism, resilience, and confidence. Use reflection to slow down and step back, to increase your self-awareness and consider your response to the commotion around you. Learn to manage negative emotions like anger, frustration, and anxiety. This will allow you to react in a more positive and productive manner and help you maintain good relationships. Having a low-key, high-performance reputation is more likely to produce positive results and to be satisfying to self and others.

Leading Others...Listen

Another "memo to self" is to listen. This has been the overarching message for leading others and building relationships. Ask questions to find out what others are thinking and concerned about. Then listen and learn.

Leading also requires following. My daughter, in a precocious moment, considering her age, reminded me that the same letters that spell *listen* also spell *silent*. It is a reminder that you can't hear what others are saying if you are doing the talking. High-performance teams are built with a commitment to each other and to learn what each member has to contribute toward the common goal.

The vision statement in one of the hospitals I worked for included *presence* as one of the core values. At first I could not understand why this was so important. Over time, I developed an appreciation for the importance of being available, to listen to and value others. This means being completely available, not multitasking while others are trying to convey important messages. It means appreciating the diversity and perspective of others and focusing on relationships first, then tasks. There is an enormous amount of research on the aspects of leadership, and their conclusions have repeated the message that successful organizations and leaders place people first.

At times, relationships with others will become challenged when conflicting goals, priorities, interpretations, methods, and values are at play. Conflict, like stress, can be either good or bad...you get to choose. Be sensitive, patient, calm, and firm when dealing with differences and disagreements in order to avoid conflict escalation. Remember that it is okay to agree to disagree but not okay to let disagreements or conflict interfere with relationships.

You have a choice to make: passive, passive-aggressive, aggressive, or assertive. Being assertive is a positive leadership characteristic. This does not mean that you will always get your way, nor should you. However, it will mean that you are being authentic in presenting your ideas, your perspective, and confidence in yourself. Reflect on your behavior and how it is perceived by others, and remember that aggressiveness or passivity are *not* exemplary leadership characteristics.

To successfully lead others, realize there is never a need to blame or shame others. When there are mistakes, delays, or other issues, look at them as learning opportunities for yourself and others. Identifying the source of the issue and how to correct it will gain more than blaming or shaming. Listening, with empathy and care, will result in stronger relationships and bonds of trust that will yield long-term results and satisfaction.

Leading Organizations...Focus on the Vision

My research on transformational leadership identified that having a vision is crucial. It is true in all aspects of life. Vision provides the direction and focus for one's organization and life. The vision and the messaging to others should be simple, easy to understand and follow, and, most of all, inspiring. Supporting priorities, goals, and objectives should be established to help in achieving the vision.

You should make decisions and plans based on their contribution toward achieving the vision. Think strategically to determine mindfully and collectively how priorities are determined and why certain decisions are made. Decisions or activities that don't provide value toward achieving the goal should be avoided or eliminated. Leadership is about effective relationship and resource management with a constant goal of focusing on the vision.

As a leader, consider how you will increase your contribution to the organizational vision. As a leader of a learning organization, ask questions to generate ideas for improvement. Also, recognize that strategy implementation can lead to conflict with established cultures and habits. This is when leaders and their change management competencies get tested. Ultimately, think strategically to create a sustainable, competitive success, and learn lessons from poor results or decisions.

Recognize that time management is not the strategy; you can't change the amount of time you have. Priority management is the strategy, choosing those priorities that will achieve your professional and personal vision. Organize your time in a strategic manner so that the long-term priorities are not sacrificed by the short-term or distracting options or choices that frequently arise.

Work–Life Integration and Synergy...Focus on Your Priorities

You get to choose what is important in your life, both professionally and personally. Be very mindful that if everything is a priority, then nothing is. As discussed many times in this book, place people first. This starts with you. Health is wealth and life is precious.

One of my graduate degrees included a focus on securities analyses, but working in healthcare I realized that my "return on investment" is enhanced by being a good steward of my body, mind, and relationships (organizational and individual). While trying to manage work priorities, I am mindful of the priorities of time with my family as well as taking time to eat, exercise, and sleep in a healthy manner. I maintain a feeling of gratitude for others around me and for what life offers. These efforts are foundational for my professional goals.

There is a frequently stated phrase: "life is good." While true, the reality is that life also includes times of disappointment, errors, setbacks, and so on. Since these are natural aspects of life, it is how you manage the bad times that determines if and how you will succeed. Remember that you have control over how you view life and its bad times. You can *choose* frustration, anger, defensiveness, or excessive behaviors and addictions *or* you can choose optimism with learning and resilience to overcome obstacles and setbacks.

Continuing the Journey

I hope that some of the observations, strategies, and advice shared in this book will be helpful to you on your leadership journey. It is intended to help you construct a personal framework for inspired actions and strategies to continue your leadership development. Different parts of the book may resonate with you depending on particular challenges you are facing. Accordingly, my hope is that the book will be helpful as a reference to assist you at different times throughout your life. The bibliography will also be helpful to you in developing your leadership capabilities on the topics covered in this book.

Reading this book is a first step; however, putting these strategies into practice is the key to achieving personal and professional success. Use the reflection questions that have been suggested throughout the book to implement your own leadership strategies to achieve excellence in leading self, others, and your organization and to reach a work–life integration and synergy.

Best of luck on your leadership journey!

Continuing Education Hours

ACMPE members who complete *Leadership Strategies: Achieving Personal and Professional Success* will receive four (4) hours of continuing education credit. Follow these directions to enter your credits online at mgma.com:

- Log in with your **last name** and **MGMA member ID#**.
- Select **My Profile** on the left side of the screen, then select **My Transcript** from the left navigation menu.
- After clicking **I Accept** on the **Confidentiality Agreement**, select the link to **Add New Credits**.
- Follow the instructions and select **Distance Learning: Assessments** for credits type, then enter the title, the date you completed the assessment, and the 4 hours.

Bibliography

American Heritage Dictionary of the English Language, various definitions, Houghton Mifflin, http://education.yahoo.com/reference
/dictionary/ (accessed May 13, 2013), 2009.

Bridges, William, *Managing Transitions: Making the Most of Change*,
3rd Ed., Philadelphia: Da Capo Lifelong Books, 2009.

Buzan, Tony, and Barry Buzan, *The Mind Map Book: How to Use
Radiant Thinking to Maximize Your Brain's Untapped Potential*,
New York: Plume, 1996.

Carlson, Richard, *Don't Sweat the Small Stuff at Work*, New York:
Hyperion, 1998.

Center for Creative Leadership, "Peter Vaill: Learning in a World
of Permanent White Water," CCL's e-Newsletter, August 2003,
http://ww4.ccl.org/connected/enews/articles/0803vaill.htm
(accessed May 4, 2013).

Christensen, Clayton M., Jerome H. Grossman, and Jason Hwang.
The Innovator's Prescription: A Disruptive Solution for Health Care,
New York: McGraw-Hill, 2009.

Cialdini, Robert B., *Influence: The Psychology of Persuasion*, New
York: HarperBusiness, 2006.

Collins, James C., and Jerry I. Porras, *Built To Last: Successful Habits
of Visionary Companies*, New York: HarperBusiness, 1994.

Collins, Jim, *Good to Great: Why Some Companies Make the Leap...
and Others Don't*, New York: HarperBusiness, 2001.

Collins, Jim, "The Stockdale Paradox," podcast, www.jimcollins.com
/media_topics/brutal-facts.html (accessed May 13, 2013), 2013.

Collins, Jim, and Morten T. Collins, *Great by Choice: Uncertainty, Chaos, and Luck – Why Some Thrive Despite Them All*, New York: HarperCollins, 2011.

Covey, Stephen R., *The 7 Habits of Highly Effective People*, New York: Simon and Schuster, 1989.

Covey, Stephen R., *The 8th Habit: From Effectiveness to Greatness*, New York: Free Press, 2004.

Csikszentmihalyi, Mihaly, *Flow: The Psychology of Optimal Experience*, New York: Harper & Row, 1990.

Csikszentmihalyi, Mihaly, *Good Business: Leadership, Flow, and the Making of Meaning*, New York: Viking, 2003.

Dannemiller Tyson Associates, *Whole-Scale Change: Unleashing the Magic in Organizations*, San Francisco: Berrett-Koehler, 2000.

Dictionary.com, Integration, *Dictionary.com Unabridged*. Random House, Inc., http://dictionary.reference.com/browse/integra tion?s=t, (accessed June 7, 2013).

Dictionary.com, Synergy, *Dictionary.com Unabridged*. Random House, Inc., http://dictionary.reference.com/browse/synergy ?s=t, (accessed June 7, 2013).

Drucker, Peter F., *The Daily Drucker: 366 Days of Insight and Motivation for Getting the Right Things Done*, New York: Harper Business, 2004.

Frankl, Viktor E. *Man's Search for Meaning*, Boston: Beacon Press, 2000.

Gladwell, Malcolm, *Outliers: The Story of Success*, New York: Little, Brown, 2008.

Goleman, Daniel, Annie McKee, and Richard E. Boyatzis, *Primal Leadership: Realizing the Power of Emotional Intelligence*, Boston: Harvard Business School Press, 2002.

Heifetz, Ronald A., and Martin Linsky, *Leadership on the Line: Staying Alive through the Dangers of Leading*, Boston: Harvard Business Review Press, 2002.

Hughes, Richard L., Robert C. Ginnett, and Gordon J. Curphy, *Leadership: Enhancing the Lessons of Experience*, Boston: McGraw-Hill/Irwin, 2011.

Kim, W. Chan, and Renee Mauborgne, *Blue Ocean Strategy: How to Create Uncontested Market Space and Make Competition Irrelevant*, Boston: Harvard Business School Press, 2005.

Kreitner, Robert, and Angelo Kinicki, *Organizational Behavior*, Boston: McGraw-Hill/Irwin, 2012.

Lencioni, Patrick, *The Five Dysfunctions of a Team: A Leadership Fable*, San Francisco: Jossey-Bass, 2002.

Liker, Jeffrey K., *The Toyota Way: 14 Management Principles from the World's Greatest Manufacturer*, New York: McGraw-Hill, 2003.

Mackay, Harvey, *Dig Your Well Before You're Thirsty: The Only Networking Book You'll Ever Need*, New York: Doubleday, 1997.

Maxwell, John C., *Failing Forward: Turning Mistakes into Stepping Stones for Success*, Nashville: Thomas Nelson Publishers, 2000.

McCall, Morgan W., Michael M. Lombardo, and Ann M. Morrison, *Lessons of Experience: How Successful Executives Develop on the Job*, New York: Free Press, 1988.

Michalko, Michael, *Thinkertoys: A Handbook of Creative-Thinking Techniques*, 2nd ed., Berkeley, Calif.: Ten Speed Press; 2006.

Northouse, Peter G., *Leadership: Theory and Practice*, Thousand Oaks, Calif.: Sage Publications, 2012.

Quinn, Robert E., *Deep Change: Discovering the Leader Within*, San Francisco: Jossey-Bass, 1996.

Schwartz, Barry, *The Paradox of Choice: Why More Is Less*, New York: ECCO, 2004.

Senge, Peter M., *The Fifth Discipline: The Art and Practice of the Learning Organization*, New York: Doubleday/Currency, 2006.

Shaw, Robert Bruce, *Trust in the Balance: Building Successful Organizations on Results, Integrity, and Concern*, San Francisco: Jossey-Bass, 1997.

Swenson, Richard A., *Margin: Restoring Emotional, Physical, Financial, and Time Reserves to Overloaded Lives*, Colorado Springs, Colo.: NavPress, 2004.

Tichy, Noel M., with Nancy Cardwell, *The Cycle of Leadership: How Great Leaders Teach Their Companies to Win*, New York: HarperBusiness, 2002.

Wells, Stuart, *Choosing the Future: The Power of Strategic Thinking*, Boston: Butterworth-Heinemann, 1998.

Index

NOTE: (ex.) indicates exhibit.

About the Author

Ronald Menaker, EdD, FACMPE, MBA, CPA, has 28 years of experience in medical group practice. Menaker is on the administrative team at Mayo Clinic in Rochester, Minn. Prior to joining Mayo Clinic, Menaker was the executive vice president of Prevea Health Services in Green Bay, Wis., and an assistant director of patient care at Marshfield Clinic in Marshfield, Wis.

Menaker received his doctor of education degree in organization development from the University of St. Thomas in Minnesota, a master of business administration in finance from the University of Wisconsin, and is also a certified public accountant. He is a participating adjunct instructor teaching leadership in the University of St. Thomas Health Care and Evening MBA programs in Minneapolis, Minn. Menaker has been actively involved in the Medical Group Management Association and the American College of Medical Practice Executives (ACMPE), serving on both Boards of Directors, and is past chair of ACMPE.